Using the Writer's Notebook in Grades 3-8

Pat,
I hope this book
helps you with
your student
writers. Good for
you for taking
on the challenge!

Good luck,
Janet

Using the Writer's Notebook in Grades 3-8

A Teacher's Guide

Janet L. Elliott
Purdue University

National Council of Teachers of English
1111 W. Kenyon Road, Urbana, Illinois 61801-1096

Manuscript Editor: Susan Campanini

Production Editor: Bonny Graham

Interior Design: Doug Burnett

Cover Design: Frank P. Cucciarre, Blink Concept & Design, Inc.

NCTE Stock Number: 35006

Library of Congress Cataloging-in-Publication Data

Elliott, Janet L., 1958–
    Using the writer's notebook in grades 3-8 : a teacher's guide / Janet L. Elliott.
        p. cm.
    Includes bibliographical references.
    ISBN 978-0-8141-3500-6 ((pbk.))
    1. English language—Composition and exercises—Study and teaching (Elementary)
2. Language arts (Elementary) 3. Creative writing (Elementary education)
4. Notebooks. I. Title.
    LB1576.E426 2008
    372.62'3044—dc22

                                                                    2008029250

For all my friends and colleagues who have been part of this journey

Contents

Acknowledgments

I never intended to write a book. I just wanted to be more successful in using writer's notebooks with my intermediate students, as well as help other teachers and students experience success. It started as a quest to find out everything I could about using writer's notebooks with young writers. I learned from professional writers and their published works, and I continue to work with and learn from students and teachers in the classroom, taking advantage of opportunities to expand my understanding. Somewhere along this path, I was encouraged (even begged) by classroom teachers to create a practical resource to help them, a resource that they could take back and use daily with their students.

This book could not have become a reality without those who have supported, guided, and nurtured me along the way. To Ralph Fletcher, Katie Wood Ray, Carl Anderson, Lucy Calkins, and other writing gurus, I thank you for being my writing mentors. Not only have your resources been immensely helpful, I have learned from your workshops and from watching you work your magic with young writers.

To Irene Fountas, Gay Su Pinnell, Jill Eurich, and others with the Literacy Collaborative, I thank you for the incredible training that I received in both primary and intermediate literacy.

To my colleagues at the Center for Literacy Education and Research at Purdue University; Maribeth Schmitt, Sarah Mahurt, Angie Schoenbeck, Shannon Henderson, and Marissa Fletcher, you have continued to help me grow by creating visions and thinking "outside the box."

To my many friends and teachers at Goshen Community schools, we have walked side by side on this journey, sometimes stumbling but always determined to help children become more successful readers and writers. Your passion continues to inspire me.

To my former students, along with teachers and students around the state of Indiana, I thank you for letting me come into your classrooms, peek inside your notebooks, and learn from you on a daily basis. You are why I've invested the time and energy into writing this book, and the things you are doing as writers keep refueling my energy.

I want to extend a heartfelt thank you to my editors at NCTE, Kurt Austin, Bonny Graham, and Susan Campanini, as well as to Cari Rich, for your help in making this book a reality and your gentle guidance and patience during the publishing process. I have learned so much!

And finally, I am grateful to my family and my husband, John, for letting me pursue my passions and be who I need to be. The hours of travel, reading, and writing that have preceded this work would not have been possible without your support.

Introduction

I now understand how other authors of books on the topic of writing must feel. It seems strange to be writing a book about writing, living the process as I write about it. Talk about making one feel a sense of inadequacy! One must quiet the voice inside that whispers, "What in the world do you think you are doing?" This voice is only silenced by the insistent voices of students and teachers, myself included, who want to grow in their expertise as writers and teachers of writing.

In this book you will find Chapter 1 helpful in thinking through the rationale for using writer's notebooks with children. Perhaps you or your colleagues wonder if it's worth the time and effort necessary to use them on a consistent basis. What are the benefits of using writer's notebooks?

Chapters 2 and 13 give you practical tips and procedures on how to use notebooks successfully with your students. These chapters guide you and help you avoid some of the problems that others have experienced. How do you get started? What do you do when a writer can't think of anything to write about? What about privacy issues?

A unit of study for the writer's notebook is presented in Chapter 8, a chapter to refer to when introducing the writer's notebook to students at the beginning of the school year.

Chapters, 3, 4, 5, 9, 10, and 12 offer a wealth of ideas for quick writes, observations, poetry, and writing across the curriculum. These ideas help you keep your notebooks active and relevant all year long.

The writing process and writer's craft are addressed in Chapters 6 and 7. Notebook writing can be developed into a writing project, and, through the writing process, the notebook can be used to plan and craft the writing.

Chapter 11 stands in a unique position—but as an integral part of all of the other chapters. Boy writers can be a challenge at times. We know the untapped potential that lies within them, and we need to give thought and consideration to the mentoring and nurturing of these writers.

It is my hope that you will keep this book at your fingertips. I want you to write in the margins, use sticky notes for ideas, and dog-ear the pages as you read. Jot down your reflections on what went well and on what you would change. Share your successes with colleagues, and don't forget to write in and share from your own writer's notebook. And remember to take time to celebrate the progress that you and your students are making as writers!

1 Why Use a Writer's Notebook?

A notebook can be the clearing in the forest of your life, a place where you can be alone and content as you play with outrage and wonder, details and gossip, language and dreams, plots and subplots, perceptions and small epiphanies.

Ralph Fletcher (1996, p. 5)

As a child, I wanted to use a writer's notebook. The problem was I didn't know how. I remember owning several diaries through the years, with entries that read something like this: "I went to school today. Nothing much happened. I worked on my insect collection after school. Still need to find a moth so will have to go outside tomorrow night." Is it any wonder that I lost interest after a week or two of these mundane entries? I certainly didn't feel as though those attempts were worth saving, so the diaries got pitched somewhere along the way.

Years later, after marriage and children, I wanted to remember what my young sons said and did as they grew through the different stages of childhood. So I tried again. I began recording humorous and touching moments in a spiral notebook. (Like the time that my five-year-old said to me, "For some reason, Mommy, you look pretty today!") Unfortunately, this notebook met the same fate as my diaries. After a few entries, it too was forgotten on the shelf, never to be written in again.

I finally broke this pattern when I learned how to use a writer's notebook. Years ago, when I received my intermediate literacy training, I was required to use a writer's notebook. Together with my peers, we explored a variety of ways to use the notebook, and we read resources that deepened our understanding of its purpose. As we shared our writing with each other, I began to realize what an important tool the writer's notebook was for me and to envision what it could be for my students.

Slowly, as I continued to write in my notebook, I began to view myself as a writer. I had thoughts, feelings, opinions, reactions, and memories to record. I became more observant of people and of my surroundings, and I began to feel the urge to write down things that previously would have seemed insignificant. I squeezed a lot of artifacts between the pages of my notebooks and wrote about the experiences that were tied to them. But, more important, I found that I did some of my best thinking when I wrote. When I had opinions, thoughts, or reactions to express, I grabbed my notebook so that I could disentangle them on paper. Some of these entries have led to letters, poems, tributes, op-eds, and other forms of published writing.

A writer's notebook can be seductive in a good sort of way. It tugs at your elbow, enticing you to write just a little about this or that—until, one day, you realize that you are living a writerly life!

Development of Self

Students need to understand the purpose of a writer's notebook. Children who are not familiar with a writer's notebook typically want to write diary or journal entries, just as I did when I was young. (Many published writers use the labels *notebook*, *log*, and *journal* synonymously, as is evident in the author quotes throughout this book. However, it is important for children to understand what a writer's notebook is used for; it is a matter of function, not label.) We must help our students understand that a writer's notebook is more than a diary. It is a place to write about experiences, observations, thoughts, and reactions. We want students to view their notebooks as a place to collect seeds by recording bits and pieces of their lives—a place to make sense of their lives and a place to savor their lives.

A Place to Record Memories

I share with students how lucky they are because they are learning to use a writer's notebook at a young age. I envy them. They will be able to tap into their childhoods for years to come, just by rereading their notebooks. I stress the importance of saving their notebooks forever.

After a few months of using a notebook, Taylor's reflection (Figure 1.1) shows that he is beginning to have a sense of what his notebook will mean to him in the future.

A Place to Savor Life

More important, we need to show our students how to savor the richness of their lives. When our children understand that a notebook serves them anytime, any place, in any circumstance, they begin to understand how the notebook helps them slow down and write about the small, everyday things that shape who they are and who they will become.

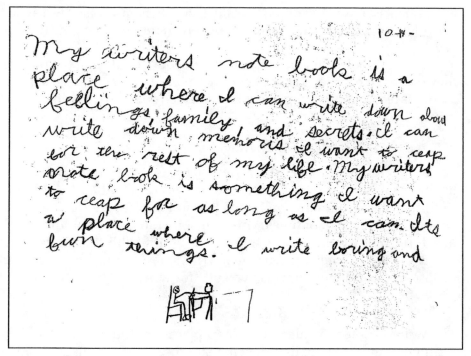

Figure 1.1. Taylor's notebook reflection.

Development of Writer

A Nonthreatening Place to Write

Students quickly learn to appreciate their notebooks as a place to write that is free of risk. No one is checking for grammar and spelling errors. A few years ago, one of my students had a classic case of writing phobia when he entered fourth grade. He followed me around with his notebook and pencil in hand. "How much do I have to write? Do I need to skip lines? Do I have to fill the whole page?" My response to him was the following: "Just write! Don't worry about how you do it. Just get your thoughts written down." Once he understood the freedom that the notebook gave him as a writer, he no longer worried about performing for me.

Young writers can write with honesty as they try to make sense of their lives. Terry Tempest Williams, writer and former teacher, found journal writing to be the single most important gift that she could give her students. "It was their time to really listen to themselves; it was when the noise stopped and the thinking began" (cited in Graham, 1999, p. 179).

A notebook also gives writers the freedom to play on the page as they explore the writer's craft or try a new genre. When there is no judgment placed on the writing, the writer is given space to experiment and grow.

A Place to Collect Ideas for Writing

Once students have collected a variety of ideas in their notebooks, they have a resource to use for writing project ideas. (See Chapter 3.) I used to cringe when students complained, "I can't think of anything to write about." I wasted a lot of time trying to inspire those who couldn't think of a topic that would be worthy of their effort. With their notebooks always at their fingertips, budding writers have a wealth of ideas to choose from, and more time is available for writing.

A Place to Plan for Writing

The writer's notebook also provides a place for students to plan their writing. They can web, list, sketch a storyboard, make diagrams, use whatever helps them organize their thoughts. Carl Anderson (2005, p. 108) refers to this step of the writing process as rehearsal. Writers have different ways in which they rehearse their writing, and each student needs to find what works for him or her.

Recently, I visited an eighth-grade classroom and was deeply troubled by some of what the students were experiencing, I wrote a poem about how the students' lives outside of school have an impact on their ability to learn. I rehearsed in my notebook by listing the scenarios (without names) and writing my reactions to them before actually writing the poem. What I will do with the poem at this point is unknown, but it is in my notebook, and I feel a little bit better as a result. I envision including it in an op-ed to vent my frustration with the pressure that educators are under to get students to perform on standardized tests, with no consideration given to the emotional or physical state that the students are in when they walk through the doors of the school.

A Place to Live Like a Writer

Most of us have a sense of where and when we learned to read. But how many of us can pinpoint where and when we became writers? Like many teachers that I work with, I don't remember writing much until I was in high school and college. A few of the lucky ones had a teacher in the younger grades who valued writing and nurtured them as writers.

The notebook encourages young writers to live like many writers do. Many published authors use notebooks. Some don't. Yet most writers use some method of collecting ideas that works for them. Writers such as Peg Kehret (2002) collect their ideas in a box. Mary O'Neill's classic poetry book, *Hailstones and Halibut Bones* (1989), was the result of a drawer full of notes, poems, and unfinished stories. For the sake of organization and convenience, it makes sense to use notebooks as the collection tool in our classrooms.

Development of Community

A Place to Learn about Our Students

At a recent workshop, Carl Anderson shared why he began using the writing workshop in the early years of his teaching career. It bothered him that he didn't know many of the students that he was teaching in middle school, and he longed for a way to connect with them. When he moved to the workshop approach, he was able to sit side-by-side with students in personal conferences. Carl was able to respond to students' writing and discuss ways to strengthen their skills. This mentor relationship helped him get to know each student on a deeper level and fulfilled the need that he previously felt.

I learn to know my students much better by listening to them share from their notebooks and by reading some of their notebook entries. I understand the interests, fears, pressures, opinions, and passions that drive them. Charlotte's pie graph (Figure 1.2) clearly shows her concern for animals.

A Place to Write with Our Students

If we expect our students to value and use a writer's notebook, we need to walk the path with them. If you don't already use a writer's notebook, begin today! Write with your students as they write. Share your entries with them. Demonstrate that you are willing to take risks as a writer, just as you are encouraging them to do. Your students will appreciate your honesty and willingness to learn alongside them, and they will learn to know you better as you share what matters to you. Students will value their notebooks more when you model the use of your notebook by writing in it authentically and frequently.

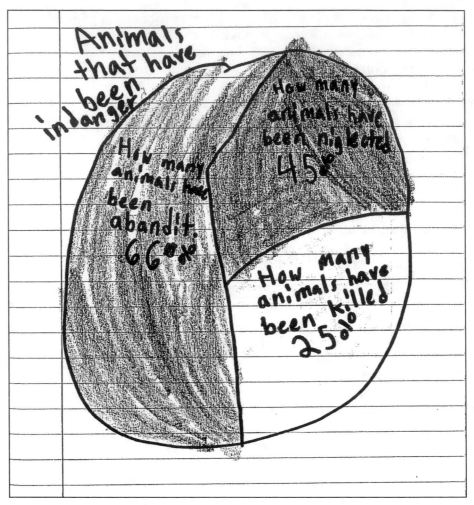

Figure 1.2. Charlotte's graph about animals.

Support for Curriculum

A Tool for Meeting Standards

Currently, many state standards and district curriculum goals encourage using a notebook to collect ideas for writing projects. The Indiana State Standards (Indiana Department of Education, 2006) for the writing process in Grades 3 through 8 include the following statement: "Discuss ideas for writing, use diagrams and charts to develop ideas, and make a list or notebook of ideas." (The writer's notebook is listed in the Standards on pages 28, 36, 46, 54, 65, and 75.)

In November 2004, the Executive Committee of the National Council of Teachers of English (NCTE) published their beliefs about the teaching of writing. (See Appendix.) These beliefs offer important principles to guide effective teaching practice. Under Principle 4, it states:

> In any writing assignment, it must be assumed that part of the work of writers will involve generating and regenerating ideas prior to writing them. Excellence in teaching writing as thinking requires that the teacher understand:
>
> - Varied tools for thinking through writing, such as journals, writer's notebooks, blogs, sketchbooks, digital portfolios, listservs or online discussion groups, dialogue journals, double-entry or dialectical journals, and others.

A Tool to Improve Writing Fluency

Frequent use of the writer's notebook improves writing fluency. Those who struggle to get even a few words on paper eventually learn to write more quickly, which results in increased amounts of writing. The more students write, the more fluid their writing becomes. Writers need to be able to record their thinking quickly before their thoughts escape them. This benefits students writing for standardized tests, when they are required to get thoughts on paper within a limited time frame.

Principle 2 from NCTE's guidelines for writing states: "The more people write, the easier it gets and the more they are motivated to do it. Writers who write a lot learn more about the process because they have had more experience inside it."

A Tool to Use Across the Curriculum

The writer's notebook is also a way to integrate writing into other content areas, such as science and social studies. It can be used in special classes, such as art and music, as students respond to information or musical and artistic experiences. Investigations can also take root in the notebook as students research a topic and record information to develop into a writing project.

In subsequent chapters, I discuss how to use and sustain the use of the writer's notebook effectively in intermediate and middle school classrooms. I want to spare you the frustration of Jean Little's sixth-grade teacher when she gave her students notebooks and asked them to record their daily happenings and feelings. After reading boring entry upon boring entry, she announced to her class, "I have never, in my whole life, read such rubbish . . . I shall never assign journal writing to a class again" (Little, 1991, p.125). What Little's teacher didn't realize was that she needed to teach the children how to use the notebook. Just putting a journal into their hands was not enough.

It is my hope that you will experience success as you explore the use of writer's notebooks with your students and that this success will continually fuel your energy and passion for this writing tool. When you understand the purpose that this tool serves and you experience the power that it holds, I will have accomplished my purpose for writing this book.

2 Getting Started

A journal should be a place to wander, to draw, to scribble, to explore. A clean page is freedom. As for size, I like them big enough to do some damage in, and small enough to carry. Quality paperback book size is my preference. I also like cool paper, hand-made or recycled. Eye-burning white is nice, crisp.

Graham Salisbury (cited in P. W. Graham, 1999, p. 39)

When I was required to take a writer's notebook to literacy training, I remember making a special trip to the bookstore to select one that was perfect for me. What a decision that was—every size, shape, color, and theme imaginable! I ended up with one that had a Monet painting with pastel shades of purples and pinks on the cover—the perfect gift to myself. This notebook is now stuffed with all kinds of writing and mementos, so I've been forced to put it on the shelf and move on to other notebooks. But that first notebook will always be special because it holds many treasures and because it proves that I actually filled an entire notebook without abandoning it! My filled notebooks have become old friends—to revisit for enjoyment, reflection, and writing ideas.

Selecting a Notebook

There are a few things to consider when introducing notebooks to your students. Do you want your students to buy their own notebooks and bring them to school? If so, encourage them to think about these things when making their selections:

- Choose a notebook that is inviting to write in. Do you want pages with lines or without lines? (Some writers even like the notebooks with graph paper.)
- Choose a sturdy notebook, something that will hold together for a long time. (Spiral notebooks don't hold up well, and students are more likely to tear out pages.)
- Choose one that is convenient to carry around.

Some teachers want the selection of a writer's notebook to be a personal choice. Others prefer to provide inexpensive notebooks because their students have limited resources. (Some schools include the cost of the notebook in their fees for materials.) I have found the composition notebooks to be affordable and durable, and they are available in a variety of colors and designs.

If your students use composition notebooks, they can decorate and personalize them by pasting quotes, photos, magazine pictures, drawings, or stickers on the front. Contact paper can also be used to protect the covers. Some students like to cover their notebooks with cloth, vinyl, or stretchy book covers to make them more attractive. (Scrapbooking materials are great for decorating.) Together with your class, explore ways to personalize notebooks and give your students the opportunity to create their own unique notebooks. The more ownership that writers feel for their notebook, the more writing they will do!

I love the way that Jean Little captures the thoughts and feelings of a young writer in her book *Hey World, Here I Am!* (1990): "Getting a journal is like buying shoes. You have to find the one that fits. And you are the only person who can tell if it pinches" (p. 74). Once you and your students find notebooks that fit your personalities, you're ready to write.

Building Anticipation

Be enthusiastic as you anticipate that first day of writing in the notebooks! Give your students a deadline of a week or two to get their notebooks purchased and personalized. Meanwhile, build anticipation by reading some entries from your own notebook and letting them share how they relate to your experiences. I like to share entries about growing up in a large family on a farm, animals I've loved and lost, or attending kindergarten and first grade in a one-room schoolhouse. By doing this, students get to know me on a more personal level and they begin thinking about experiences that have shaped their lives.

How can you get started writing in your own notebook? You can start by selecting some of your favorite writing ideas in the following chapters. Invite some of your peers to get together over coffee to write and share. This will generate even more ideas and give you a sense of how it feels to be in a community of writers. Your excitement will grow as you collect meaningful entries and learn to know your colleagues in a deeper way. Your enthusiasm will be contagious as you model for your students. Write and share from the heart and your students will learn to do the same.

Show your students how writers work by reading from resources that tell how authors collect ideas for their writing. (Chapter 8 gives more detail in a unit of study on the writer's notebook.) A resource I especially like is Ralph Fletcher's paperback, *A Writer's Notebook: Unlocking the Writer within You* (1996), which was written for young writers. I read aloud excerpts from his book when I introduce what a writer's notebook is and how it is used. I continue doing brief introductions to a variety of children's authors so that students can learn about their writing habits. Eventually, I turn author talks over to the students and they become part of the writing workshop structure, taking a couple minutes at the beginning of the workshop, several times a week.

I share my own notebook journey and I tell students how I wish I had begun using one at a young age. To be able to read my entries from my grade school years would be like going back in time. I have snippets of memories from years ago that I've been able to hold onto, but what a gift it would be to read my thoughts and feelings from the days of my youth. I tell my class that the good news is I can give them this gift by helping them establish this writing habit now.

In *Speaking of Journals* (Graham, 1999), Bruce Coville shares the explanation that he gives students. He tells them that there are some ugly truths about their lives and one of them is that everything fades.

> There's probably not one of you here who can tell me in detail what happened your first day of first grade, a very important day in your life, but it's all recorded in your under brain. It's all registered there, and there is a way to save it and that's by keeping a journal. Journal keeping is a way of saving your life, saving yourself for yourself, a gift you give yourself, a gift you give yourself ten years later. (p. 191)

How many of us can recall experiences such as kindergarten graduation? As a third grader, Brittany is still able to recall how she felt on that day. (See Figure 2.1.) A kindergarten graduation card from her grandparents—an artifact that she glued in her notebook—was the catalyst for writing about this memory.

Setting Up Guidelines

As soon as we begin using notebooks, I say to the students: "Fifth graders, this year we are going to use writer's notebooks to help us live like writers. In order to do this we need to set up some guidelines that will help us." I talk them through some of the basic guidelines and explain why they are important, because notebooks may be new for many of them. We construct a chart to revisit when necessary or to add to throughout the year, as more guidelines are needed. This chart is displayed in the classroom for easy reference or revision.

Some helpful guidelines are the following:

- Have your notebook close at hand so that you can write in it often. Keep it in a safe place.

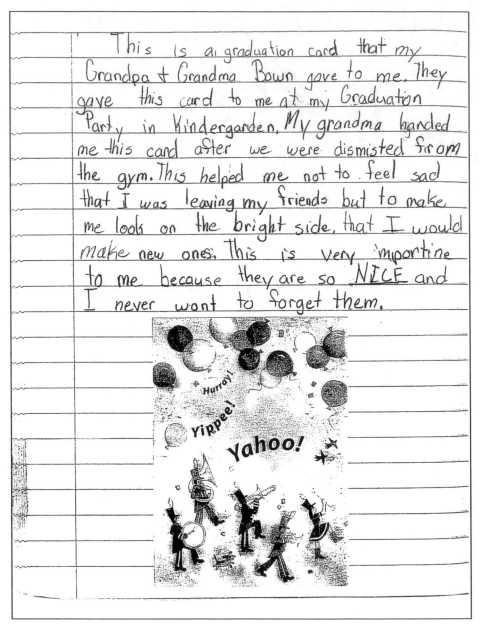

This is a graduation card that my Grandpa + Grandma Bown gave to me. They gave this card to me at my Graduation Party in Kindergarden. My grandma handed me this card after we were dismisted from the gym. This helped me not to feel sad that I was leaving my friends but to make me look on the bright side, that I would make new ones. This is very importine to me because they are so NICE and I never wont to forget them.

Hurray!

YIPPEE!

Yahoo!

Figure 2.1. Brittany's entry about kindergarten graduation.

- Write your name and the name of your school on the inside cover in case you lose it.
- Begin a new entry on the next clean page or leave enough white space after each entry in case you want to write more about that topic at a later date.
- Date your entries. When you reread your notebook, you will want to know when you wrote the entries, especially years from now.
- Cross out; don't erase. Erasing slows down the flow of writing. Don't try for the perfect notebook—this is more about taking risks as a writer. Also, you will have a record of your thinking if you don't erase, and it may be something you want to use in the future.
- It's okay to make mistakes. Spelling and punctuation are not the focus—it's more important to get your ideas down on paper. Use your knowledge about writing, but don't get hung up on conventions.
- Don't tear anything out; don't throw anything away. You never know when you might want those ideas, down the road.
- Never criticize your writing. Don't allow that voice inside your head to tell you that your writing is no good. It doesn't have to be a masterpiece, just honest writing.
- Respect the privacy of others by not reading their notebooks without permission.

Some guidelines that we've added later in the year are the following:

- When you begin a new notebook, keep your filled notebook at school so that you can return to it for writing ideas.
- Work in your writer's notebook during writing workshop when you aren't working on a writing project or when you want to plan some writing or try a revision technique.

Guidelines are for you and your students to create and use so that the notebooks can be used effectively. Incorporate whatever ideas you need to make them work.

Creating a Community of Writers

It's important to build a community of writers, promoting trust and support as we help each other become stronger writers. (If you've ever shared your writing with an audience, you know that writing is personal, and sharing it with others often conjures up feelings of insecurity and vulnerability.) The most effective way to teach this is to model respect and sensitivity as you interact with your students. At the beginning of the year, I tell my students: "This year, we are going to help each other grow as readers and writers; we are here to help each other learn. Each of you has your own personal strengths and needs. Everyone progresses at a different rate, but by helping each other we can all reach our goals."

Sharing is so powerful, as writers learn to know each other in deeper ways. By listening to each others' writing, we learn what our peers like or dislike, what they value, what their struggles are—who they are as people. We share laughter and tears as we learn more about who we are through the sharing of our life experiences.

By sharing, we also glean more ideas for our own writing. Creating an "Ideas for Writing" page at the back of the notebook gives writers a place to jot down quickly any new ideas that have been sparked from the sharing of their teacher or classmates. It is powerful to know that the writing I shared has prompted listeners to think of something that they could write about—that I helped them as writers.

Nurturing the Writer

At the beginning of the school year, we do lots of writing in our notebooks before moving into a writing workshop. One of my goals is to free students of any writing anxiety that they may carry into the classroom. Some students initially plead, "Do I have to write?" "How much do I have to write?" "Is half a page enough?" My reply to them is the following: "Just write!" It doesn't take long for them to realize that their notebooks are a safe place to write, with few requirements. Quick writes (defined in Chapter 5) only take a few minutes, which is usually manageable for even the most reluctant writer. Students write one or more entries daily for the first month or so, and we ease into a sixty-minute workshop when the notebooks have "a feeling of fullness" (a term that Katherine Bomer uses) in order to provide fertile ground for future writing.

I wish I could assure you that all of your students will fall in love with notebook writing the first day you begin. However, that isn't realistic, and you would feel discouraged if some students moan when they "have to" write. We've been writing in our notebooks for over a month now and I'm just beginning to feel that the fifth graders I'm working with are getting into a rhythm; they are just beginning to unwrap the gift that I am giving them. At first, you may see writing that is difficult to accept, either in quantity or quality. Bite your tongue, affirm what you can, and nudge them forward. The payoff will come later.

3 Planting Seeds

Most of the basic material a writer works with is acquired before the age of fifteen.

Willa Cather (p. 20)

As I work with classroom teachers, I often hear them lament that their students just haven't had many experiences to write about. Whenever I hear this, I share with them Frank McCourt's powerful words: "Nothing is significant until we make it significant" (p. 1). All children have experienced life—perhaps not in ways we would choose for them, but they are participating in life. It is our job to validate their lives by honoring their thoughts, feelings, and daily experiences whether or not they fit with our preferences or values.

Lucy Calkins writes in *Living between the Lines* (1991):

> We cannot give youngsters rich lives. We cannot give them long family suppers full of shared stories, rainbow-colored markers and sheaves of drawing paper, photograph albums full of memories, and beautiful picture books lined up beside their beds. We can't give children rich lives, but we can give them the lens to appreciate the richness that is already there in their lives. Notebooks validate a child's existence. (p. 35)

When we help children view their lives in meaningful ways, they can begin recording strands of their unique lives in their notebooks.

What Is a Writing Seed?

One of Webster's definitions for the word *seed* applies to this writing metaphor: the source, origin, or beginning of anything. (Lucy Calkins and others associated with the Teachers College Reading and Writing Project were the first to use the term *seed* to describe a notebook entry.) A seed may or may not grow into a writing project, but a variety of seeds are collected in the notebook so that writers have a storehouse to choose from when they want a writing project to take root. In this chapter (and in Chapters 4 and 5), you will find a variety of ways to gather seeds with your students.

The Value of Planting Seeds

You may be wondering, "Why not save time and just give writers topics or prompts to respond to?" Just as we need to work up the soil around a seed to allow it to germinate, the same applies to planting seeds in a notebook. Ideas need to be talked about and shared to get thoughts flowing. They need to be open-ended so that writers aren't confined to a narrow topic that they can't relate to. The more ideas writers have to choose from in their notebooks, the more likely they are to find a topic in which they are willing to invest time and energy to develop. When writing becomes personal and meaningful, half the battle is won with reluctant writers.

Writing with Honesty

Anne Lamott says, "The very first thing I tell my students on the first day of a workshop is that good writing is about telling the truth. We are a species that needs to understand who we are." (1995, p. 3)

I began to understand Lamott's statement when I wrote an entry in my notebook about an incident I had long forgotten—or at least thought I had forgotten (see Figure 3.1). This buried memory surfaced during my training, when we were exploring childhood memories. I had never told anyone because I was ashamed and didn't want to admit that I was capable of such an act.

Later, as I developed this seed into a memoir, I realized that I had learned something important from this incident (see Figure 3.2). It was painful to admit that I had stolen something—yet powerful to realize that the lesson I learned had stayed with me for a lifetime. When I share this with students, they are always amazed (if not a bit shocked) that a teacher could steal, even at a young age. Honesty in writing, as we reflect on our actions and reactions, can result in deeper understanding of who we are.

Effective Ways to Generate Ideas

Create Webs

Web "Fear," or another concept that your students can relate to, in the following ways:

- With your students, construct a web (on a white board or chart paper) with "fear" in the middle. Ask for ideas of things that people fear; add spokes to the web as they contribute.
- Ask students to make their own "fear" webs in their notebooks.
- Have them circle one that they want to write about.

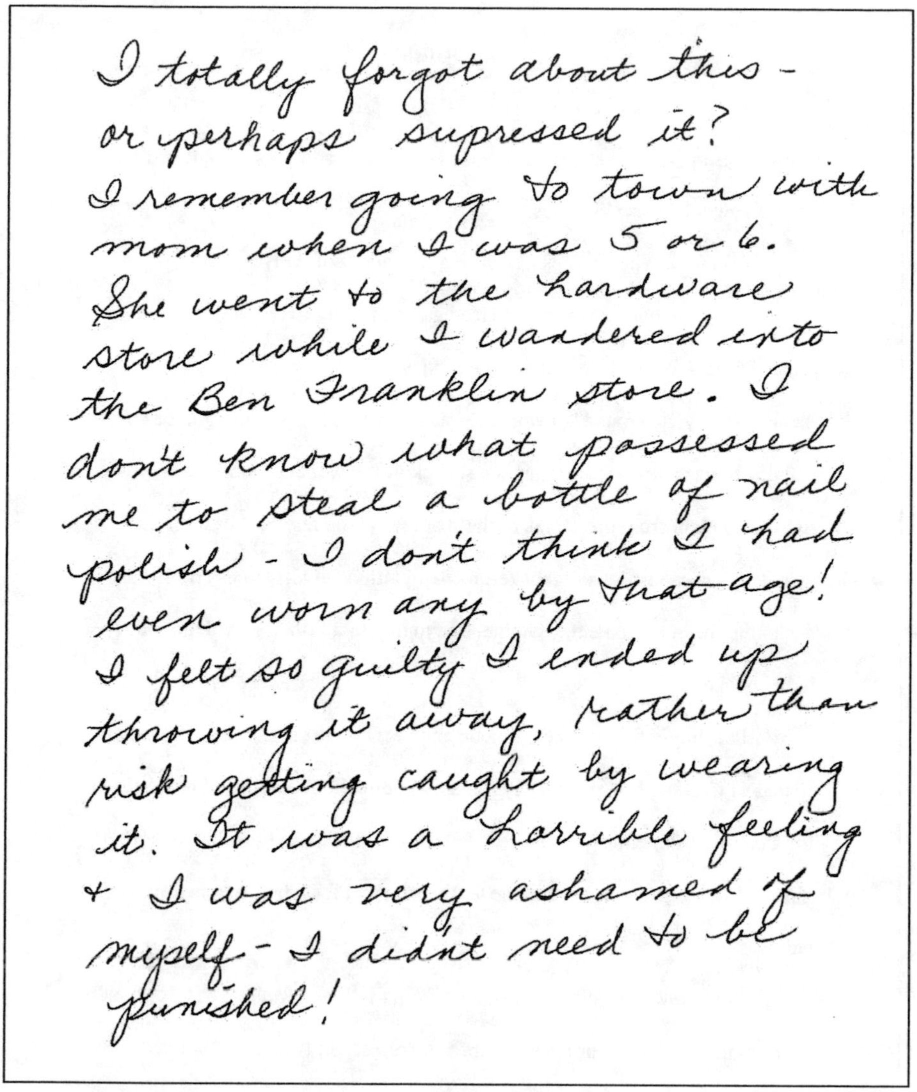

I totally forgot about this -
or perhaps supressed it?
I remember going to town with
mom when I was 5 or 6.
She went to the hardware
store while I wandered into
the Ben Franklin store. I
don't know what possessed
me to steal a bottle of nail
polish - I don't think I had
even worn any by that age!
I felt so guilty I ended up
throwing it away, rather than
risk getting caught by wearing
it. It was a horrible feeling
+ I was very ashamed of
myself - I didn't need to be
punished!

Figure 3.1. My notebook entry about the nail polish.

- Quick write (three to five minutes, depending on the grade level; younger children may need more time).
- Students share only the topic that they wrote about so that sharing moves along quickly.
- Students record any additional ideas, generated from hearing others' topics, on their "Ideas for Writing" page in the back of their notebooks.

The Nail Polish

The screen door slapped the heels of my sandals as I entered the dimly-lit Ben Franklin store. Ceiling fans whispered softly as I wandered up and down the deserted aisles.

I fingered a bag of jacks, stroked a Barbie's soft velvet evening gown and turned over a Mr. Potato Head game in order to check out the price. $2.95 – Wow! That was a lot of money.

"Is anyone around?" I wondered as I quickly took another glance up and down the aisles. I was certain the squeak of the wooden floorboards would summon a clerk from the depths of the shadows at the rear of the store.

Toys, candy, jewelry, make-up…temptations in all shapes and sizes, beckoning for me to take them home. Beckoning to a little girl with no money in her pocket.

Pausing in front of the cosmetic counter, I gazed into a sea of color: all shades of lipstick, face powder, eye shadow. Something compelled me to reach for a bottle of fingernail polish. Rose Petal Blush I read on the label. Shades of pink swirled together as I rolled the bottle back and forth between my moist palms.

Somehow, the nail polish slipped from my grasp and into the front pocket of my sundress. The floorboads groaned in protest as I turned and walked slowly out the front door, scarcely breathing.

Thud! The screen door slammed shut behind me, mocking the pounding deep within my chest. The deed was done, but the guilt lingered overhead like a thundercloud on a stormy day. I threw away the nail polish, I never told anyone, and I never did *it* again.

Figure 3.2. My published memoir about the nail polish.

You can provide more direction by giving students the categories for the web spokes. For example, the spokes of "Fear" might include these topics: People I Fear, Weather, Animals, Losing Something, and so on. Then students can make a list under each spoke. The more spokes and lists there are, the more ideas the students will generate.

Ask students to create a list of topics for other webs that they could make. Have students share one; again, students can add more ideas for webs to their own lists.

Here are some examples of student ideas:

- memories of food
- surprises
- pets
- friends
- school
- family
- heroes
- weather
- music
- nature
- celebrations
- sports
- clothes
- birthdays

Figure 3.3 shows the web that Alex made about his friend Jake. He generated many potential topics just from this web.

Create Lists

Brainstorm ideas for lists, such as the following:

- ways I like to relax
- things that are hard for me
- things I love
- things that annoy me
- things that are gross
- things that make me happy
- things that are peaceful
- irritating sounds
- mistakes I've made

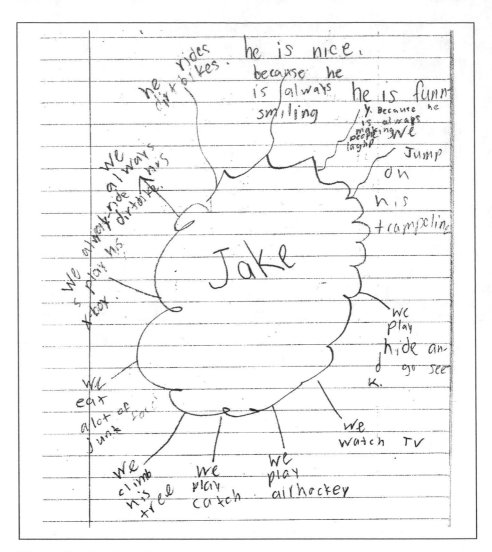

Figure 3.3. Alex's web.

You can extend by asking students to circle a topic that they want to make a list for and then give them several minutes to write. Share ideas with the whole group or in small groups. Figure 3.4 is a list of things that make Alyssa feel good.

In Figure 3.5, Hanna made a list of ten reasons why she loves her cat. Lists such as Alyssa's and Hanna's can be organized into Top Ten Lists; this is easier to do after the original list has been written.

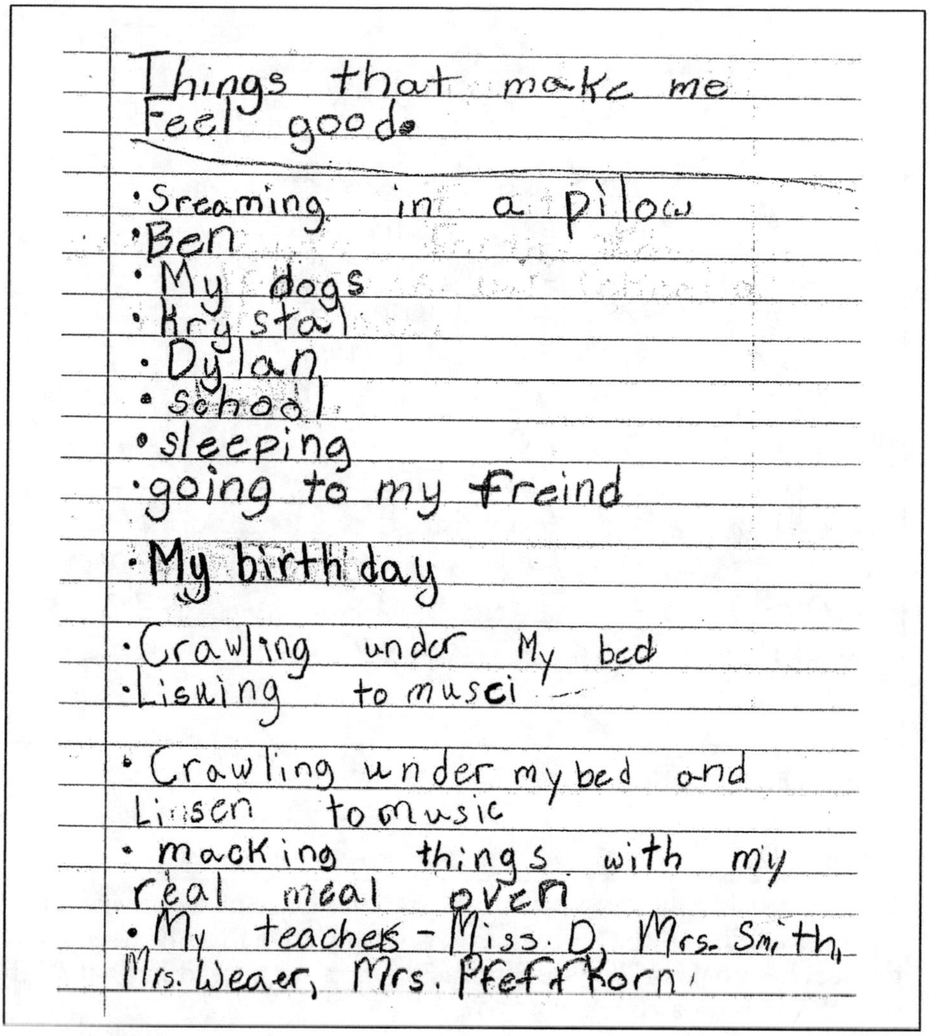

Things that make me Feel good.

- Sreaming in a pilow
- Ben
- My dogs
- Krystal
- Dylan
- school
- sleeping
- going to my freind
- My birthday
- Crawling under My bed
- Lisning to musci
- Crawling under my bed and Linsen to music
- macking things with my real meal oven
- My teachers – Miss. D, Mrs. Smith, Mrs. Weaer, Mrs. Pfeffkorn

Figure 3.4. Alyssa's list.

More Ideas for Lists

Five New Things You Want to Do or Try

1. Eat a new kind of food.
2. Watch a sunrise.
3. Shop at a new store.
4. Ride a horse.
5. Volunteer for the Humane Shelter.

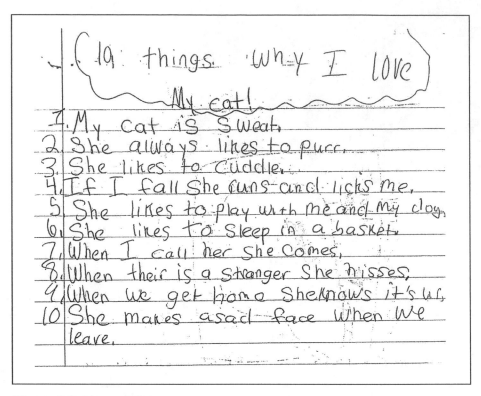

Figure 3.5. Hanna's list.

Things to Do

This is probably the most practical list that we use on a daily basis. Already as a third grader, Carol has her list of things that she needs to do to meet her goals in life (see Figure 3.6). Be sure to read her list all the way through for a chuckle!

People I Admire

Student writers make a list of people they admire and can then choose a person to write about. It's always helpful if you share with your students first. Tell them about someone you know who has overcome challenges and has been an inspiration to you.

How has this person faced his or her challenges?

What kind of character does he or she have?

What do you admire about him or her?

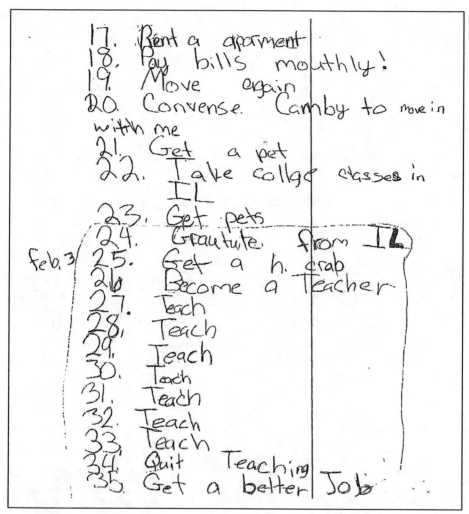

Figure 3.6. Carol's list.

Like Charlotte, students can write about someone they read about, know personally, or have seen on television (see Figure 3.7).

Things You Love or Hate

Students quickly make a list of 100 things they love. What are the little things that make them smile? What makes them happy to be alive?

Linda Rief's graphing idea in her book, *Vision and Voice: Extending the Literary Spectrum* (1998, p. 47), is a great way for students to rank their likes and dislikes (see Figure 3.8).

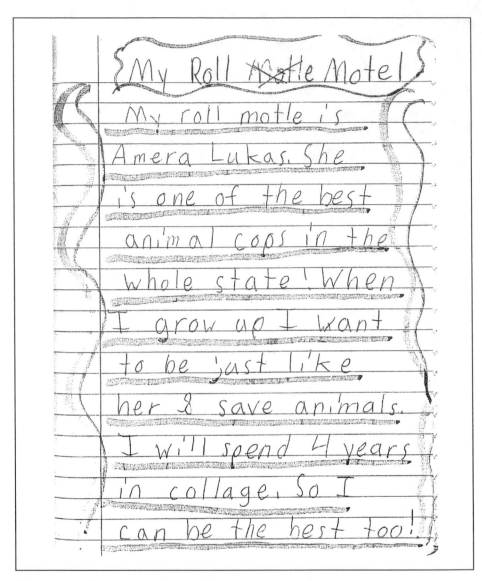

Figure 3.7. Charlotte's role model entry.

Give Me Five

This is a different format for a list. Students trace around one hand and write five things (on the fingers) that they want others to know about them or five things they don't think others know about them. This is great for the beginning of the year when you are learning to know each other.

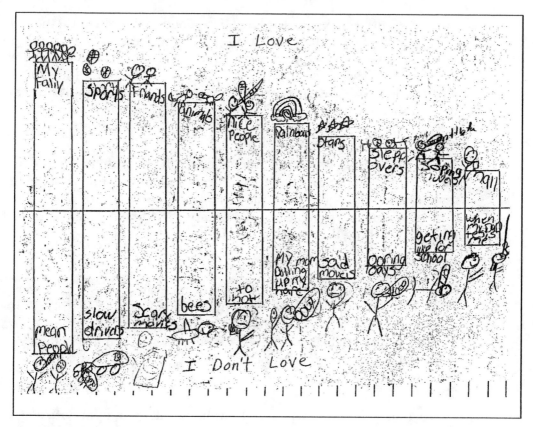

Figure 3.8. Marissa's graph.

For other ways to use the traced hand, students can list five things that they

- have either touched or done,
- learned about a certain topic,
- wonder about a certain topic, or
- don't want to do.

Create Maps

Life Maps

A colleague begins the year with her fifth graders by showing them how to make life maps in their writers' notebooks. A life map is similar to a timeline but looks more like a meandering road than a straight line. (Allow the life map to span over two pages of the notebook.) Students put the significant events that have happened in their lives on the line, starting with their birth and working up to the present. They can write a phrase or sketch a simple picture beside the dates that they list (if they know them). They can return to this life map throughout the year for writing ideas. (It's great if parents can help their children recall and chart the significant events in their lives.)

Job Maps

This is fun to do with older students or adults because they have had more work experience. Ask them to draw a job map, similar to the life map, and plot their jobs, from their first job up to their current job. They can choose one job to write about, perhaps the worst or best day of that job, or something that they learned from that job.

Maps of Special Places

In the front of Ralph Fletcher's book of memoirs, *Marshfield Dreams: When I Was a Kid* (2005), he drew a map of the neighborhood that provided such rich childhood memories. This is a great way for young writers to tap into their experiences. Figure 3.9 shows the map that Alex drew of his school neighborhood.

Quotes

I love quotes. I admire writers who can stimulate thought with so few words. Before I began using a writer's notebook, I had a small spiral notebook where I recorded all of the quotes I ran across that I didn't want to forget. Now I record them in my writer's notebook and jot down my thoughts and reactions.

Here are a few quotes that I like to use with students:

> One of my teachers told me, "Never let a day go by without looking on three beautiful things." I try to live up to that and find it isn't difficult. The sky in all weathers is, for me, the first of these three things.
>
>   David McCord (cited in Cullinan, 1996, p. 3)

I ask students to list three beautiful things that they've seen that day and choose one to write about. It is helpful to give them a "heads up" beforehand so that they are more observant of the beauty around them.

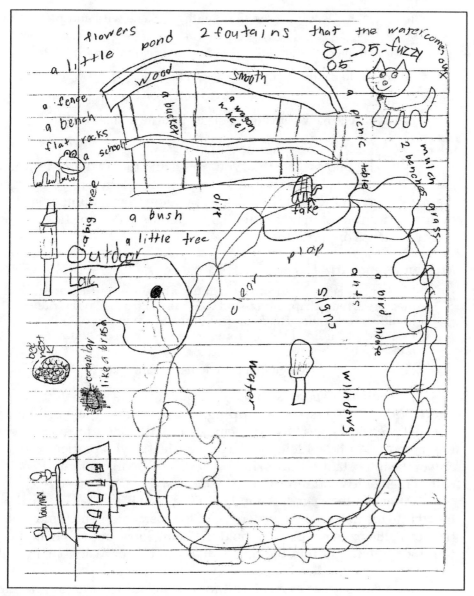

Figure 3.9. Alex's neighborhood map.

To be nobody but yourself in a world which is doing its best to
make you like everybody else means to fight the hardest battle
which any human being can fight and never stop fighting.

e. e. cummings (www.quotationspage.com)

Tell me, what is it you plan to do with your one wild and precious life?

Mary Oliver ("Summer Day" in *New and Selected Poems*, 1992)

You must do the thing you think you cannot do.

Eleanor Roosevelt (www.quoteopia.com)

I don't have to blow out your candle to make mine shine brighter.

Anonymous

Watch for quotes that strike you. You'll find them in some unusual places. Be sure to jot them down in your notebook before you forget them. I've been known to scribble down a quote from a bumper sticker on the car in front of me (at a stoplight, of course). I keep sticky notes handy for these opportunities.

Mementos and Artifacts

My journal is the heart of my writing. There I record dreams, memories, funny happenings and wild ideas. Free to play, I write in different directions and colors; I draw, I tape in leaves, notes from kids, boarding passes. From such compost, poems, stories, and even novels grow.

George Ella Lyon (cited in Janeczko, 1999, p. 2)

Did you ever keep a scrapbook of memorabilia when you were a child? Pictures, newspaper clippings, ticket stubs, sports ribbons, crushed prom corsages? I kept them all. What I didn't preserve were the memories of how I felt, details of the friends who participated, or any of the important specifics. In a writer's notebook, you can do both: collect mementos and record your memories.

A memento or artifact can be a tangible object that is glued or taped into the notebook. If writers want the memento to be removable, they can glue in an envelope to hold the item. Sometimes an item is either too large to put into the notebook or no longer available: in that case, the writer can sketch a picture of it.

Mementos serve as a catalyst for our memories. I enjoy sharing two special quilts that my grandmother made for me. One quilt was a wedding gift many years ago and the other one is a baby quilt that was given to me at the birth of my first son. This sharing immediately reminds students of their favorite baby blanket, stuffed animal, or other treasures. Encouraging students to sketch first may help them recall more details.

Photos

Photos are great to use in the writer's notebook. Photographer Joel Meyerowitz (1985) says, "Photographs are fragile paper timeships, dusted with information." Ask your students to bring photos from home to glue into their notebooks (or slip into an envelope that is glued on the notebook page) so that they can write about what's happening in the picture, the setting, or who or what is absent in the picture. Most students really enjoy writing about photographs, and it's a great way for teachers to learn about students and their families.

At the beginning of the school year, I like to take a photograph of each student to glue into the front of their notebooks so that they can write an entry about themselves. This personalizes their notebooks and helps us get better acquainted. I encourage students to steer away from the typical information in favor of writing something that others may not know or may find intriguing.

Digital pictures taken at recess, in the classroom, on fieldtrips, and at assemblies also provide notebook writing opportunities, as students select ones that they want to write about. In the older grades, you may be able to assign the job of photographer to a responsible student who is interested.

Sketches

Sketches are quick and simple—easy enough for even the most reluctant artist. There may be times when you want to encourage more detailed drawings so that writers can notice more or think more deeply about the topic. It is important for students to know the difference between sketches and more detailed drawings and the purposes they serve.

When writers sketch or draw, they think more deeply about that person or object. Sketch a neighbor, friend, teacher, or member of your family. You might describe appearance, personality, likes, dislikes, odd behaviors, things said, and more. Charlotte chose to draw and describe her ballet teacher (see Figure 3.10).

Students can sketch one of their favorite places to go to be alone. Suggest that they describe it in detail: sounds, smells, what it looks like, and more.

They might also sketch an object in the classroom or in their house. They could write for five minutes about that object—whatever comes to mind.

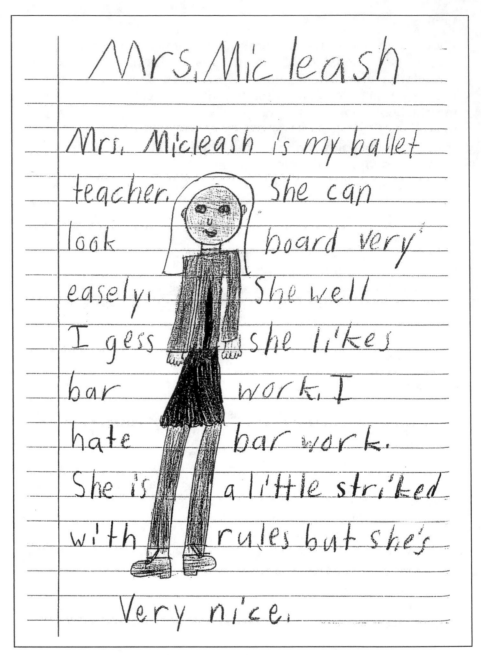

Mrs. Micleash

Mrs. Micleash is my ballet teacher. She can look board very easely. She well I gess she likes bar work. I hate bar work. She is a little striked with rules but she's Very nice.

Figure 3.10. Charlotte's ballet teacher.

Wonderings

There are many wonderful question-and-answer books in print today. Reading excerpts from books such as *How Come?* by Kathy Wollard (1993) demonstrates how curiosity can lead to writing, perhaps even research. Some of the questions posed in Wollard's book are the following: Why are bubbles round? How did the zebra get its stripes? What is a black hole?

Ask students to write down three things that they wonder about. Have them do this daily for several days to get them in the mind-set of wondering. This naturally leads into investigations (which are discussed in Chapter 12).

Newspapers and Magazines

Newspapers and magazines are great resources for articles, quotes, cartoons, editorials, and pictures. Personal responses can be written to clips that are glued into notebooks. Encourage students to choose clips that stir some emotions or reaction—something that they care about or have an opinion about—that they want to express.

Clip individual words, phrases, and headings from newspapers and magazines and keep them in a box for students to choose from. (Older students can do this for you.) When writers use these as catalysts, they often write about topics that they wouldn't have thought of exploring. The phrase that Christian selected led him to do some deep wondering, as you can see in Figure 3.11. The phrase that Brittany selected prompted her to reflect on her love of clothes and a recent experience she had with them (see Figure 3.12).

You can also request that students save pictures from newspapers and magazines. Give each student a page protector to put in the writing folder. Throughout the school year, allow students to cut out pictures of interest and slip them into their page protectors. If students need an idea to write about, they have the option to choose a picture from their collection.

Additional Ideas for Writing

- Dreams (sleep dreams, daydreams, dreams for the future)
- A scar (How did you get it? How did you feel?)
- Sleeping away from home for the first time
- A time when someone lied to you or you lied to someone
- A special day you would like to create (Kindness Day, Pets Day, Backwards Day)

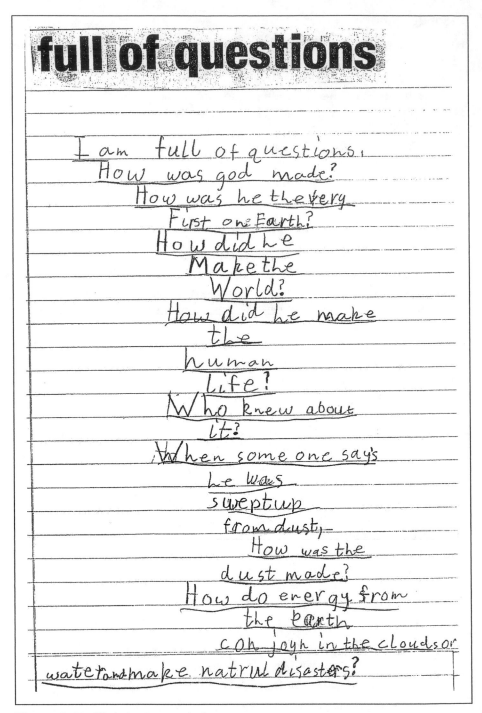

Figure 3.11. Christian's wonderings.

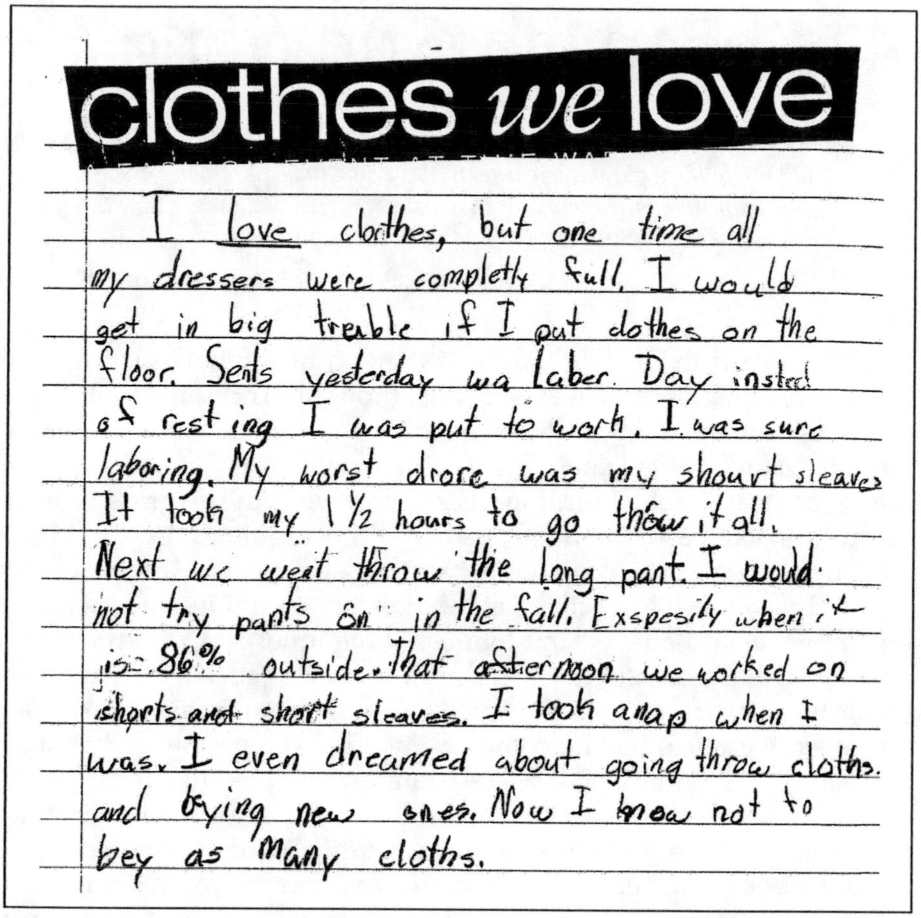

clothes *we* love

I love clothes, but one time all my dressers were completly full. I would get in big treuble if I put clothes on the floor. Sents yesterday wa Laber. Day instead of resting I was put to work. I was sure laboring. My worst drore was my shourt sleaves It took my 1½ hours to go theru it all. Next we went throw the long pant. I would not try pants on in the fall. Exspesily when it is 86% outside. That afternoon we worked on shorts and short sleaves. I took a nap when I was. I even dreamed about going throw cloths. and bying new ones. Now I know not to bey as many cloths.

Figure 3.12. Brittany's reflection on clothes.

- A vitamin you would like to create in order to make our world a better place

As you read this chapter, perhaps you thought of some ideas of your own. When you find something that works well with your writers, jot it down in your notebook so that you don't forget it. You and your writers are limited only by your imaginations!

4 Observing Our World

Nothing takes the place of keeping a journal, in which to record observations and thoughts, a phrase, a word, an idea that can be used when there is leisure time to write; nor is there any substitute for observation: the time taken to carefully examine and respond to the world around us.

Myra Cohn Livingston (cited in Janeczko, 1999, p. 10)

As I read the author's note at the end of my new picture book, *Crawdad Creek* (Sanders, 2002), I thought to myself, "I could have written this!" Scott Russell Sanders gives his readers a glimpse into his childhood. "I spent much of my childhood outside, exploring the woods and fields, turning over rocks, lying in the grass to watch clouds or stars, tracking deer, peering at flowers and bugs, drinking in through all my senses the living, breathing world" (p. 32).

Life on the farm offered all of these opportunities and more. I remember spending hours outdoors, making mud pies with rock chips, exploring our grove of trees, and trying to domesticate orphaned animals like baby raccoons. Like Scott, we owned no television until I was in seventh grade. I had no computer, no video games, no cell phone to distract me. Entertainment was seldom provided—I had to create it.

How I wish all children had the chance to explore their world with freedom and wonder. Seymour Simon, author of many wonderful nonfiction books, also began his exploration as a young child, but in a very different setting. He was born in the Bronx and lived in an apartment building. Across the street was a vacant lot that contained weeds and trees, wildflowers and insects, birds and bugs. Simon feels as though he grew up "a country kid as well as a city kid" because of the opportunities that this vacant lot offered (Simon, 2000).

Using Our Senses

The good news is that we can help our students observe and appreciate their surroundings, wherever they live. Well-known poet Bobbi Katz encourages us to "Get in the habit of quietly observing and experiencing the world around you. Trust your five senses to lead you to ideas, which are everywhere, just waiting for you to connect with them—and make them your own" (cited in Janeczko, 1999, p. 74).

Going Outdoors

It is important for our young writers to know that their everyday observations and explorations are exactly the type of powerful stuff that makes good notebook entries. Take children outside in any season and have them record their observations. By dividing a page into fourths, they can categorize their observations into sight, touch, smell, and sound. Or they can sketch and record their observations for the same scene each season.

Our school is located on a busy intersection and students first notice the obvious—traffic, tooting horns, and pedestrians walking on the street. However, with guidance, some begin to notice the leaves swaying in the breeze, the bugs crawling in the prickly grass, the smell of meat cooking on a grill—small details that previously went unnoticed.

An observation can be more focused, depending on your purpose. Ask children to record their observations when examining something outdoors, such as the bark of a tree or the bricks on the side of the school building. Encourage them to use comparisons and descriptive words. David observed lots of things as he sat in the outdoor courtyard in the middle of his school (see Figure 4.1).

Encourage your students to experiment with the following:

- Touch or feel an object.

  How does if feel? Bumpy, smooth, rough, sticky?

- Close your eyes to concentrate on listening.

  What sounds do you hear? Is the sound similar to some other sound you've heard? Is it shrill, irritating, soothing? How does it make you feel?

- Close your eyes to focus on smells.

  What smells do you notice? Are they familiar? Do they remind you of something you've smelled before? Are they pleasant or unpleasant?

- Focus on one thing to really see it. Try to get close enough to notice the tiny details so that you can write them down or sketch them.

  What features does it have? Does it resemble something else? What are the colors, shapes, lines?

- If appropriate, taste it.

  Is it sour, sweet, salty, bitter? Does it taste like something you've tasted before?

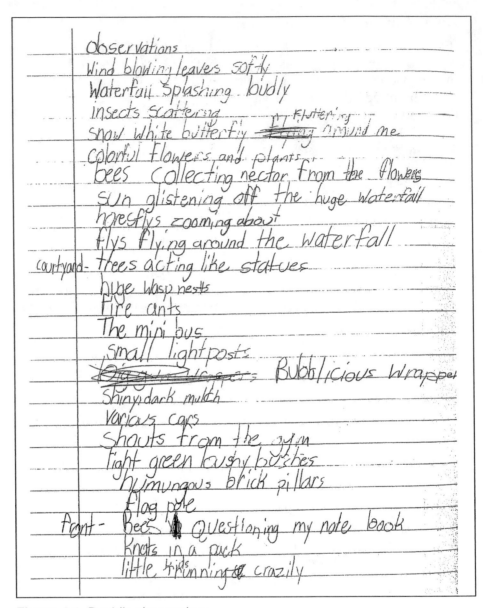

Figure 4.1. David's observations.

Not every observation lends itself to using all five senses, but we can encourage our young writers to use appropriate ones and help them strengthen their sensory observation skills.

A great read-aloud that demonstrates the power of observation is *Snowflake Bentley* by Jacqueline Briggs Martin (1998). This fascinating biography tells the story of William Bentley's passion for nature in the early 1900s. His tireless efforts resulted in photographs of snow-flakes, spider webs, insects, and other intricate works of art. The author includes a quote of Bentley's at the end of her book: "The average farmer gets up at dawn because he has to go to work in the cow yard. I get up at dawn, too. But it is because I want to find some leaf, hung with dew; or a spider web which the dew has made into the most delicate ropes of pearls" (p. 32).

Bentley's own book, *Snowflakes in Photographs* (2000), reveals the intricate beauty of hundreds of flakes, no two alike. Included are photographs of dew on such things as vegetation, spider webs, caterpillars, grass, flies, and grasshoppers.

Jim Arnosky's book, *Sketching Outdoors in Winter* (1988), is written especially for young observers. He narrates his nature discoveries and gives the reader practical sketching tips: "As you look at a nest, try to identify the various materials it is made of. Birds use grasses, pine needles, twigs, mosses, leaf parts, animal fibers, and even spiderwebs in their nests. Sharpen your pencil point for drawing fine materials such as hairs and spiderwebs. Use a duller point when sketching coarse and fibrous mosses, twigs, and grass blades" (p. 14).

Nature All Year Long, by Clare Walker Leslie (2002), is also a wonderful book to share with children. As an artist and naturalist, she captures the seasonal changes in the Northeast by drawing and writing about the uniqueness of each month of the year. Her detailed drawings demonstrate the skill of attending to the intricate details of tree buds, insects, birds, and other creatures. She encourages her readers to become more observant by giving them tasks to do.

Staying Indoors

If you can't take children outside to observe, bring nature inside— ordinary and not-so-ordinary items for students to touch, feel, smell, taste, and sketch. For small group observations, I've provided such things as lemons or oranges (sliced crosswise), fossils, an ostrich egg, peacock feathers, a rabbit pelt, shells, sand, acorns, gourds, or flowers. Be sure to provide a few magnifying glasses for close scrutiny.

Invite students to bring in their favorite nature objects, such as a shark's teeth, rocks, bird feathers—whatever treasures they have collected at home. Ask them to share why the object amazes them and why it is important to them. Encourage peers to ask questions. Each student sketches his or her own item, making sure to note the intricate details. (A word of warning: you never know what they might bring in. One year a boy brought in a squirrel's tail—when he pulled it out of the bag, we discovered that it was covered with maggots. Needless to say, it went back into the bag very quickly!)

In *Awakening the Heart: Exploring Poetry in Elementary and Middle School* (1999), Georgia Heard suggests making a window frame on one of your windows, using strips of construction paper. Observers describe in their notebooks what they see through that frame. (Only a few students do this at a time.) You may be thinking, "There is nothing interesting outside our windows!" I urge you to give it a try. You will be surprised at what your writers notice.

A few years ago, our fourth-grade classroom was located on the second floor, facing a street of parked cars. Outside our window there was one tree with a hole in the trunk. Jenae and Sophia wrote about the mystery of what lived in that hole. Brian wrote about the squirrels that he watched scamper across the street (see Figure 4.2).

These exercises in observation have caused me to be more observant of my own surroundings. One spring morning I was working in my office at school when I noticed that the branches on the tree outside my window were bobbing up and down. I sneaked over to the window to take a closer look, and, to my surprise, it was loaded with fat-breasted robins that were migrating. (I counted more than forty robins.) They were hopping from branch to branch, enjoying the dried berries that were still clinging to the tree. Every now and then, they swooped across the street to the telephone wire and then back for more berries. All of a sudden, a robin flew into the window and fell to the ground, half-dazed. This went on for several hours. I emailed the staff to let them know of this unusual sighting, and a colleague emailed back to inform me that the robins were getting intoxicated from the fermented berries. Little did I know that those robins were having a "happy hour" right outside my window! I took a few minutes to record this springtime celebration in my notebook.

Observing People

Watching

In *Nothing Ever Happens on 90th Street* by Roni Schotter (1997), Eva's writing assignment is to write about what she knows. So she sits on the stoop with an open notebook, waiting for something to happen in her neighborhood. What evolves is a wonderful story with colorful characters from the neighborhood. (Schotter skillfully leaves the reader won-

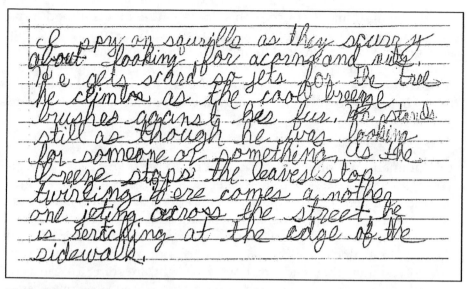

Figure 4.2. Brian's window observation.

dering when reality turns into fantasy.) Students can copy Eva by sitting on their doorstep or at a window to record observations of their neighborhoods.

Encourage your students to be people watchers everywhere they go. A friend recently found her brother-in-law's notebook in the back seat of her car after dropping him off at the airport. Scribbled in his notebook were observations that he had made about his seatmate on a long flight to Africa. He used phrases like "Big hockey fan—unbridled enthusiasm for EVERYTHING. Very very fun guy. Dirty fingernails." His detailed observations have inspired me to jot down my observations in my notebook when I travel.

Listening

Another way to become more observant in our world is to listen in on snippets of conversation (with discretion, of course). All of us have times when we can't help but overhear what people are saying to one another. In *A Writer's Notebook: Unlocking the Writer within You* (1996), Ralph Fletcher calls it, "snatches of talk" (p. 55). He encourages writers to sit down in a public place and listen to the "cadences of ordinary talk" (p. 62). Learn to listen on the playground, at the store, at a restaurant, at the football game—wherever there are people, there will be talk!

The first time that I tried this, I was eating at a fast food restaurant in Cambridge. As I munched on my salad, two employees got into an argument, not caring that their childish behavior was enough to wilt my lettuce. I jotted down the gist of the argument and my feelings about their rudeness and ended up writing a poem for two voices (see Chapter 10) in my notebook about the negative and positive aspects of words.

The Way Writers Work

I recommend a wonderful book by Peg Kehret, *Five Pages a Day: A Writer's Journey* (2002). She shares her experiences as a writer and how she incorporates her life experiences and observations into her stories. She tells about overhearing two obnoxious sixteen-year-olds outside traffic court one day: "The more they talked, the more angry I became. Finally I took a pencil and small notebook out of my purse and wrote down everything they said. You boys, I thought, are going to be in a book someday" (p. 139). Sure enough, their dialogue appeared in a scene in her book *Cages* (2001)—with the language cleaned up, of course!

An article in the local newspaper told how John Grisham was planning to write a book about politicians instead of his typical subject of lawyers. He shared how he took detailed notes during bull sessions with his fellow lawmakers during his years in the Mississippi House of Representatives. Grisham planned to use these notes to write his new book—in order to give it authenticity. Even the best of writers borrow from the conversation around them.

As writers we must learn to really look, listen, touch, taste, and smell. When we fine-tune the view of our world, we discover so much that was previously overlooked. As we develop a greater awareness of our surroundings and record the details, we gather great material to use in future writing.

5 Using Children's Literature

If I hope for literature to matter personally to them, then I need to demonstrate, encourage, and assist them in writing "from the gut" their immediate and visceral reaction to the text, often right after they read. The writing I sponsor, then, supports and guides the thinking I want to educate into their reading lives. Sometimes that thinking centers on memories the story brings up in them and reflections on those remembered events; other times the thinking is more freely associative. My instructions to them are usually to write "just what the text makes you think about, how it makes you feel, what it reminds you of, your honest first thoughts that in your head run alongside the words of the text."

Randy Bomer (1995, p. 109)

The first time I read Tomie dePaola's book *Tom* (1993), I was immediately reminded of my childhood. As Tommy helped Grandpa Tom sift the ashes from his coal furnace, I was four years old once again, watching my father shovel coal into the leaping flames of our coal furnace in the basement of our farmhouse. When Tom showed Tommy how to manipulate the feet of a butchered chicken, I knew exactly how it felt to pull those cordlike tendons and watch the claws slowly curl in. However, it never occurred to me to paint the claws with nail polish and sneak them to school to scare my classmates like Tommy did—which is probably a good thing!

Literature has an impact on readers in different ways. It connects us to past experiences, stirs our emotions, and causes us to react, wonder, or chuckle. We are so fortunate to teach in a time when a plethora of children's books is available. A variety of genres fills the shelves of the children's section at the bookstore: poetry, biographies, autobiographies, realistic fiction, fantasy, traditional literature, and informational books. Give me a little time to browse and I will walk away with a fat stack of books and a thinner pocketbook. I confess that I sometimes live by Erasmus's words, "When I get a little money I buy books; and if any is left I buy food and clothes" (www.brainyquote.com).

When we read wonderful books aloud to a classroom of young children, it isn't long before they are waving hands in the air, anxious to share their comments and experiences. We need to continue this kind of sharing and discussion as we read to students of all ages, in order to show them the kinds of connections and thinking that they can write about.

You Have to Write (Wong, 2002) is a great book to read to your children when you're exploring everyday topics to write about. "No one else can say what you have seen, and heard, and felt today. . . . Write about fights. Write about holes in your socks, your grandmother cracking her knuckles, your father snoring all night long" (p. 8). Janet Wong weaves in examples as she encourages readers to write about the dark times and the bright times. Her book helps writers realize that their daily lives are full of rich writing material.

In this chapter are many titles that work well as springboards for writing about a variety of topics, along with some suggestions for using these books. Some stories are thought provoking, others are just plain fun. Balance the serious topics with some light-hearted ones in order to keep the notebook enjoyable.

Writing about Memories

In recent years, writing about memories has grown in popularity and many authors are publishing their memoirs. Even struggling writers can write about themselves or about something that they've experienced because they know the plot and how it unfolds.

Share powerful examples of memoir with your students and discuss the differences between memoir and a memory. (Many writing experts refer to these exemplary texts as *mentor texts*.) A memory recalls what happened, whereas a memoir includes the reactions, thoughts, and emotions that accompanied that memory, and a memoir is usually written in the first person, to give the reader a more intimate perspective. In her book, *Writing a Life: Teaching Memoir to Sharpen Insight, Shape Meaning—and Triumph over Tests* (2005), Katherine Bomer defines memoir in detail and explains how to help students write effectively in that genre. Her book is especially helpful for developing a seed into a memoir writing project.

My Favorite Mentor Texts for Teaching Memoir

Chapter Books

> *Marshfield Dreams: When I Was a Kid* by Ralph Fletcher
>
> *Looking Back: A Book of Memories* by Lois Lowry
>
> *A Girl from Yamhill* by Beverly Cleary
>
> *Small Steps: The Year I Got Polio* by Peg Kehret
>
> *When I Was Your Age: Original Stories about Growing Up* (Volume 2) edited by Amy Ehrlich

> *Boy: Tales of Childhood* by Roald Dahl
>
> *But I'll Be Back Again* by Cynthia Rylant
>
> *The Circuit: Stories from the Life of a Migrant Child* by Francisco Jiménez

Picture Books

> *White Water* by Jonathan and Aaron London

(Note: the following three books are written in English and Spanish.)

> *In My Family/En mi familia* by Carmen Lomas Garza
>
> *Family Pictures* by Carmen Lomas Garza
>
> *My Tata's Guitar* by Ethriam Cash Brammer

Books That Spark Memories

Fireflies! by Julie Brinckloe

> The thrill of catching a jar full of fireflies is contrasted by the boy's guilt as he watches them beat their wings against the glass and fall to the bottom as he tries to fall asleep.

Connections to this book could be as simple as catching fireflies or as complex as letting go of something you cherish.

The Summer My Father Was Ten by Pat Brisson

> Each spring as they plant the garden, a father tells his daughter the story of the summer he was ten and he and his friends got carried away during a baseball game and ended up destroying Mr. Bellavista's garden. This incident led to a lifelong friendship between the boy (her father) and Mr. Bellavista.

Discuss family stories with your students, stories that parents have told them, stories that students want to tell their own children someday. Writers make a list of family stories and choose one for a quick write.

When I Was Young in the Mountains by Cynthia Rylant

> Rylant shares her memories of living in the mountains with her grandparents. Simple and repetitive text is great for younger children.

Make a list of memories that you have with your grandparents or other relatives. Choose one to write about.

Memories Triggered by Senses

Senses are powerful catalysts for remembering our past. Smells that trigger memories for me are popcorn (a Sunday evening snack for our large family when I was growing up) and the Old Spice that my father dabbed on his neck after he shaved.

Sights and sounds can also reconnect us to the past. Have you ever heard a song that took you back to a certain era, place, or relationship? It's all stored in your mind, waiting to be awakened and recorded on paper.

Books with Sensory Connections

"The Long Closet," a story by Jane Yolen (in Erlich, *When I Was Your Age*)

> Yolen recollects the smells associated with her grandparent's closet—cedar, mothballs, and her grandfather's sweat. Her grandmother didn't have a signature odor until she was all alone and "had taken to sucking on lemons" (p. 62).

What smells trigger memories for you? What do you remember about that person or place?

The Hickory Chair by Lisa Rowe Fraustino

> Louis has been blind from birth but that doesn't keep him from playing hide-and-seek with Gran. He can always sniff her out because "She had a good alive smell—lilacs, with a whiff of bleach" (p. 3). He loves the touch of her warm face and her salty kisses. These memories carry Louis through the worst moments after she is gone and he feels forgotten.

Writing about Holiday Memories and Traditions

Traditions are important and every family has them. Read aloud some of these books to begin a discussion about the various traditions that your students' families have.

The Christmas Gift by Francisco Jiménez

> Francisco's migrant family experiences a difficult winter in a farm labor camp in California. All that he can dream of for Christmas is a red ball. He learns that there are more important things that can bring joy.

What traditions do you celebrate each year? What special memories do you have of past Christmases?

The Christmas House by Ann Turner

> Each room of the house is filled with special memories that are told from different viewpoints in poetic form.

What would your house say about your holiday events and traditions?

One Candle by Eve Bunting

> A traditional Hanukkah celebration has a deeper meaning as Grandma and Great-Aunt Rose tell their story each year. This story of perseverance during the darkest hours of the Holocaust is interwoven with the traditions that have become so important to the family.

What stories and traditions have been passed down in your family?

Writing about Names

Names are of personal importance to children and there is usually a story or two behind every person's name (see Figure 5.1). This is a great topic for the beginning of the year, when you and your students are learning to know each other and are building a community of writers.

Whole-class discussion after reading segments of these books will give writers many ideas for angles from which to write.

- How did you get your name?
- Have you ever been called nicknames?
- How do you feel about your name?
- What do you wish you had been named?
- Have you ever been teased about your name?
- What does your name mean? Does the meaning fit you?
- Who are you named after?
- What stories do you know about family members' names?
- Have you ever chosen a pet's name? How did you decide on the name?

Books That Inspire Writing about Names

"My Name," a story in *The House on Mango Street* by Sandra Cisneros

> This short story is for older students. Sandra writes about how she got her name, how people pronounce her name, and what she would rather to be named.

My Name Is Maria Isabel by Alma Flor Ada

> Maria Isabel bravely faces her first day at a new school, but when she meets her new teacher, she is told that there are already two other Marias in the class. Her teacher wants to call her Mary instead, unaware that Maria was named for both of her grandmothers, a grandfather, and her father. Maria's inability to respond to the name Mary leads to more problems that eventually get resolved.

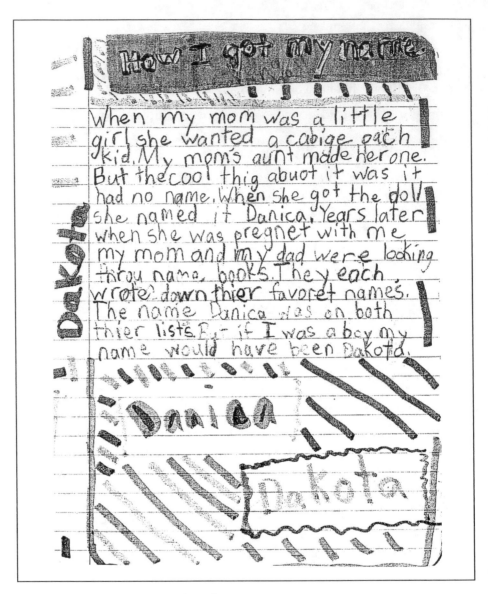

Figure 5.1. Danica's entry about her name.

My Name Is Yoon by Helen Recorvits

> This story depicts a Korean girl's difficult adjustment to her new life in America. Yoon decides that her name looks much happier written in Korean than in English. In the end, she comes to accept both her English name and her new American self, recognizing that, however her name is written, she is still Yoon.

The Name Jar by Yangsook Choi

> Unhei, who has just come with her family from Korea, is starting school and feels awkward about her name after some teasing on the school bus. She decides to choose an American name, and her classmates help her by filling a glass jar with their suggestions. Her mother reminds her that she and her grandmother went to a name master for Unhei's name; in the end, Unhei finally decides to keep her name.

Gooney Bird Green by Lois Lowry

> In Chapter 2, Gooney, a hilarious storyteller, shares with her second-grade classmates how her loving parents came up with her unusual name.

Writing about Special Places

Most children desire a space of their own so that they can get away for time alone. When I was young, I remember walling off a space in our attic with boxes so that I could retreat to my hideaway with books and toys. In *My Very Own Room*, Amada Pérez (2008) writes about finding a space all her own in a house that hosted her large family and many transitional families.

Students may have a special place outdoors or at a relative's house. When I attended country school in first grade, we had a huge lilac bush in the schoolyard. We managed to clear a space in the middle of the bush, and I spent many recesses playing there with friends.

In Ralph Fletcher's book of memoirs (*Marshfield Dreams*, 2005), he includes a detailed map of the neighborhood where he grew up. He has labeled significant sites such as the woods he loved to explore and the mud puppy place in the swamp. The settings for his memoirs are sketched on his map.

More Books about Special Places

A Quiet Place by Douglas Wood

> "Sometimes a person needs a quiet place" (Wood, 2002, p. 1). A young boy imagines lots of possibilities—such as the woods, the desert, or by the sea. He ends up deciding that the best quiet place is when he is reading, thinking his own thoughts, and feeling his own feelings.

The Secret Place by Eve Bunting

> Bunting tells the story of a city boy who finds a secret place that is the home for many kinds of urban wildlife. He enjoys visiting this wonderful place during the day and at night.

All the Places to Love by Patricia MacLachlan

> This beautifully illustrated book reminisces about an era when family had time for the simple pleasures in life. Everyone in Eli's family had a favorite place—his favorite place is the marsh "where ducklings follow their mother like tiny tumbles of leaves" (MacLachlan, 1994, p. 24).

Writing about School

School is something that every student has experienced. When I read Avi's book, *The Secret School* (2001), I immediately thought about the one-room schoolhouse that I attended for kindergarten and first grade. As I read, more memories surfaced, so I quickly jotted them down in my writer's notebook. I wanted to remember those forgotten details so that I could write about them more extensively in the future.

Books about School Experiences

Sister Anne's Hands by Marybeth Lorbiecki

> Sister Anne is the new second-grade teacher and Laura loves how she makes learning fun. However, Sister Anne encounters prejudice, and the way that she handles it is an inspiration to all readers, young and old.

Thank You, Mr. Falker by Patricia Polacco

> What an impact Mr. Falker made on Patricia's life. Without his intervention, she never would have learned to read. Patricia recalls the words that he spoke to her and his physical appearance. "He was tall and elegant. Everybody liked his striped coat and slick gray pants—he wore the neatest clothes" (Polacco, 1998, p. 17).

This true story is a great springboard for writing about influential teachers, coaches, or anyone who taught your students something in the past. Students could also write physical descriptions of former teachers, idiosyncrasies, personality traits, and more.

Writing about Friends

Children usually find it easy to write about friends because they've had lots of experiences with them, both happy and sad. Discuss friendship with your class to give the students some ideas for writing.

Ideas for Writing about Friends

Make two lists: Places I Have Friends and Special Friends. List all of the places where you have friends, such as church, clubs, school, neighborhood, sports, and so on. List the special friends that you have in these organizations or places. Choose one friend to write about.

Encourage students to help generate categories such as the following for webs:

- things I do with my friends
- making a friend
- losing a friend
- problems with friends
- friends I'll always remember

Students copy the list in their notebooks and then make a web with words or phrases under each category. Circle one of those categories and write about it. (This helps students write with a more narrow focus.)

Books about Friendship

Rosie and Michael by Judith Viorst

> Written in humorous poetic form, this book is a great read for two voices. Rosie and Michael alternate voices, each telling why the other person is his or her friend.

This is fun for two students to read aloud. Be sure to read the poem and author's note at the end of the book.

Enemy Pie by Derek Munson

> It was the perfect summer until Jeremy Ross moved in down the street and became neighborhood enemy number one. Luckily, Dad had a sure-fire way to get rid of enemies. However, part of the secret recipe is spending an entire day playing with the enemy, which results in a newly formed friendship.

Students can write about experiences that they've had with enemies, bullies, or conflicts with friends.

Freedom Summer by Deborah Wiles

> This story of friendship between two boys of different races takes place during the turbulent 1960s. Joe and John Henry want to do everything together, and they are excited that they are finally allowed to swim in the town pool together until they find out what some white folks have done to prevent that from happening.

This is a powerful book and one of my favorites! Student writers can connect to making friends with someone who was different from them in some way and note the challenges or rewards.

Writing about Pets

I could write a book about all of the pets that I've had in my lifetime. Recently, I made a list in my notebook of all of my pet experiences, and I was amazed at all of the animals that I have survived. This entry made me realize that I could probably be labeled as an animal lover!

As a child, I tried to raise everything from orphaned baby raccoons to baby mice. (My mother nixed the baby mice idea; the baby raccoons, Ricky and Racky, unfortunately didn't make it, in spite of my nurturing efforts with a doll bottle.) I managed to survive a variety of pets that my boys had while they were growing up, as well as several classroom pets.

A week ago, we put down our fifteen-year-old Dachshund, Oscar, which was a very difficult decision for our family. My notebook writing has been cathartic as I work through my feelings of loss. Animals provide so many rich experiences to write about, even the sad times.

Books about Pets

My Cats Nick and Nora by Isabelle Harper

> Every Sunday afternoon, Isabelle and her cousin Emmie play with Nick and Nora. The cats try to hide so that they can avoid being dressed in doll clothes, taken for buggy rides, and made to play school.

Barry Moser's wonderful illustrations in this simple book capture the essence of the cats' personalities!

Nibbles and Me by Elizabeth Taylor

> In this reprinting (2002) of a 1946 edition, Elizabeth Taylor tells the delightful adventures of her beloved pet chipmunk, Nibbles.

The Tenth Good Thing about Barney by Judith Viorst

> A young boy deals with his grief by thinking of ten good things about his dead cat.

This is a great book for helping young writers cherish the memories of pets that they have lost.

Writing about Family

There are many wonderful books about family relationships and issues that can be read as springboards for writing. Experiences can range from the birth of a sibling to visiting an elderly grandparent.

Books about Family

The Pain and the Great One by Judy Blume

> At the beginning of this story, big sister expresses her frustration with the preferential treatment received by her little brother. Then, midway, the point of view changes, and little brother gives his perspective, which of course is very different.

Anyone with siblings can relate to this story.

The Memory String by Eve Bunting

> Laura has a string of buttons that help her remember the mother that she lost. She doesn't really hate her step mom, but she isn't happy that Jane married her dad. The tension between Laura and her step mom is realistic, and the resolution is heart warming.

Students can write about challenges that their family has encountered.

Sunshine Home by Eve Bunting

> Timmie's grandmother broke her hip and is recuperating in a nursing home. When he and his parents visit her for the first time, Timmie notices how his parents are pretending to be cheerful. In coping with this difficult situation, this loving family learns to be open about feelings.

Students may have experience visiting an elderly relative. Have they ever visited a nursing home? What did they think, feel, and smell? How do they feel about the way that old people are treated?

"Always Wear Clean Underwear!" and Other Ways Parents Say "I Love You" by Marc Gellman

> This is a fun read for any age! Gellman writes about the legendary sayings that parents use to raise children. According to the author, each saying has a little meaning and a big meaning.

What sayings do your students' parents always use? What do students think their parents are really trying to say or do? Will the students say these things to their own children some day?

Writing about Feelings and Moods

Let's face it. Some days are better than others. Our emotions are influenced by daily events and physical well-being. These books can help children write about their feelings and reactions.

The Way I Feel Sometimes by Beatrice Schenk de Regniers

> Students can identify with these poems about feelings. "I'm warning

you, stay out of my way. Today's my day for being mean mean mean!" (*Mean Song*, 1988, p. 10).

Who hasn't had days when they've felt like this?

What Are You So Grumpy about? by Tom Lichtenheld
> This book pokes fun at being a grump and gives lots of funny excuses for irritability.

The end covers consist of sketches and sure cures for grumpiness. The illustrations are great!

Once When I Was Scared by Helena Clare Pittman
> Ted Rands's illustrations enhance this story of a boy who lives in the mountains and is sent to get hot coals from the neighbors. When daylight fades, Daniel's imagination soars and he manages to conquer his fears on his journey home.

What fears do your writers remember having as young children? What fears do they currently have? Have their imaginations ever run wild?

Courage by Bernard Waber
> Waber's simple book explores the many kinds of courage—the awesome kind and the everyday kind. "Courage is not peeking at the last pages of your whodunit book to find out who did it. Courage is being the first to make up after an argument" (2002, p. 15).

Encourage students to write about something that they do, or have done, that takes courage or to write about someone that they know who is courageous.

The ideas in this chapter (as well as Chapters 3 and 4) will aid you in planting a variety of seeds during the first several weeks of school. Continue to use these ideas or similar ones in order to keep notebook writing thriving all year long. As you gain more experience, you will discover additional opportunities for writing that haven't been mentioned. Keep your eyes and ears open for texts and other opportunities that lend themselves to notebook writing. When writer's notebooks become fertile seedbeds, you are ready to help your students select ideas from their notebooks and to take them through the writing process.

6 Developing a Notebook Entry

Workshop is a rigorous learning environment that has roots in the traditional system in which apprentices learned the skill of their trade by working at the sides of master craftsmen and women.

Fletcher & Portalupi (2001, pp. 2–3)

I f you had peeked into my classroom years ago, you would have seen students with their heads bent over their desks, diligently writing on a daily basis. However, at that time I knew little about the structure of a writing workshop. Some very important components were missing, so I didn't achieve the results that I could have with a workshop approach. I didn't know how to present a focused minilesson and reinforce my teaching point during conferences and group sharing. Since then, I've learned how to maximize student learning by using the three parts of a writer's workshop: minilessons, conferring, and sharing.

Writing Workshop

Writer's workshop, originally developed by Donald Graves, requires a predictable time each day to write, sixty minutes if possible. Students need to know that they will write every day, so that they can anticipate the work that writers do and get into a rhythm that supports their writing processes.

These sixty minutes are divided into the following activities:

- a brief minilesson (5–10 minutes)
- independent writing and conferring (40–45 minutes)
- sharing (5–7 minutes)

Minilessons

Words that play over and over in my head when I plan minilessons come from Lucy Calkins and her colleagues at the Teachers College Reading and Writing Project.

> Often it feels weird to end our minilesson. We know they don't "get" it yet. But we need to remember that our saying words isn't ever going to mean we are teaching anyone to do anything. We need to send the kids off to work in order for them to have an

opportunity to do the learning. They'll do the learning as they write, read, work. They need to make something of what we've said.

                                                        Lucy Calkins (1994, p. 15)

Stating a minilesson in one or two sentences helps me narrow my focus and forces me to use concise statements. I think about what my writers need to learn, and then I write it on chart paper, a whiteboard, or overhead transparency. The written minilesson statement is a visual way for students to attend to the learning focus because it is easy for some listeners to daydream and not listen to what you are saying.

Independent Writing and Conferring

During independent writing time, students write as I confer with individuals or work with a small group of students with similar needs. As a mentor, I sit beside my students in order to talk with them about the writing work that they are doing. I teach into their writing, helping them learn more about the revision and editing processes. Carl Anderson's book, *How's It Going? A Practical Guide to Conferring with Student Writers* (2000), is a great resource for learning more about the roles of student and teacher as they work side by side.

Sharing

Time slips away if I don't keep one eye on the clock, especially when students are deeply engaged in their writing. It's tempting to drop the sharing time in order to allow just a few more minutes to write, especially if students groan when the workshop comes to a close. (Believe me, this does happen!) I'm reluctant to break the spell. However, I've come to realize that, if I skip sharing, I lose 50 percent of my teaching and learning potential. Sharing isn't just a time to bring closure to an hour of writing; it's a time to check, clarify, and reinforce understanding of the minilesson, and it's an opportunity for writers to learn from and celebrate with each other.

The Writing Process

Donald Murray is credited for identifying the steps that writers go through in order to develop a piece of writing. Additional writing experts, such as Nancy Atwell (1998), Lucy Calkins (1994), and Ralph Fletcher (1996), have deepened (and continue to deepen) my understanding of this process.

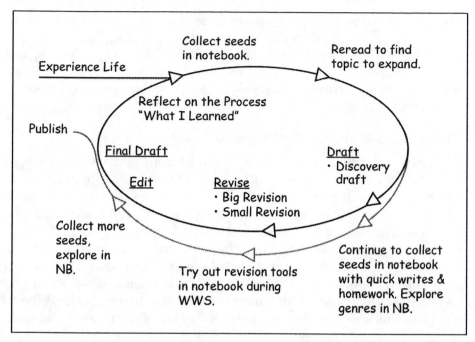

Figure 6.1. The writing process.

If you feel inadequate as a writer or teacher of writing, let me reassure you that you will become a more skilled writer as you teach your students about the craft of writing. Consider it an opportunity to learn on the job, to walk hand in hand with your students as you learn together. Your students will appreciate your honesty and willingness to take risks along with them.

Figure 6.1 (adapted from Bomer, 1995, p. 84) shows the cycle through which writers move.

To say that writers move through this exact sequence step by step would be simplistic and misleading. Writing is an individual process, and all writers need to find a process that works for them. What works for one writer may not work for another. However, this chart is helpful for teaching the stages that writers go through in some fashion. We need to help students understand that writing is a recursive process—that we often spiral back as we compose our thoughts, write them down, and revise what we have written.

Figure 6.1 also demonstrates how the notebook continues to be an integral part of the writing process throughout the year. A few minutes can be devoted to quick writes several times a week so that additional ideas can be gathered. Students continue to use their notebooks as a *workbench* (a term borrowed from Randy Bomer) as they try out revision tools in their notebooks. When waiting for a conference or after completing a writing piece, students can explore genres and topics in their notebooks.

Choosing an Idea from the Notebook

After spending four to six weeks at the beginning of the school year gathering a wide variety of entries, how do writers go about developing an entry into a writing project? First of all, allow students adequate time to read over their notebook entries and attach a sticky note to a couple entries that they are interested in developing. They should choose topics that they care about so that they are willing to invest more time and energy. Demonstrate this process using your own notebook and think aloud about some of the entries that you want to develop. (If you have a genre focus, ask your students to choose entries that lend themselves to this specific kind of writing. I find it easier to teach the writing process before beginning a genre study.)

Discovery Draft

After narrowing the notebook choices to one entry, students close their notebooks and write down everything that they can think of regarding their topic. If their notebook entry contains powerful and memorable writing that they want to use in their discovery draft, they may want to refer to their notebooks. However, some writers may try to copy the entire entry. When this happens, there is nothing new to discover—it's simply an exercise in copying. The purpose of the discovery draft is just as its label implies: it is an opportunity to dig deeper and uncover more thoughts, details, feelings. It is truly an act of discovery.

In a discovery draft, students are free to let their thoughts flow through their fingertips, without worrying about conventions or craft. They are expected to use what they know about writing, but the focus is to put thoughts down on paper. When writers skip lines, it leaves room for revision and editing. It's helpful to use different colored paper for discovery drafts and final drafts. This makes it easy to see what stage of the process students are in as you move about the room.

Revision

Once discovery drafts are written, the next step is revision. Our students' writing informs us of what our writers need to learn about the craft of writing. Do they need minilessons on focus, details, leads, endings, voice, word choice, sentence fluency, or organization? You may be answering yes to all of these. Choose several minilessons to teach within one project. Rest assured that, if something is a problem in one piece of writing, it will show up again in future pieces and you can address it then. Don't make the mistake of trying to make a piece of student writing perfect. The process is more important than the finished product—we are teaching the writer, not trying to perfect his or her piece of writing.

Ralph Fletcher and Joann Portalupi have published several resources that are helpful in teaching students the craft of writing.

Craft Lessons: Teaching Writing K–8 (Fletcher & Portalupi, 1998)

Nonfiction Craft Lessons: Teaching Information Writing K–8 (Portalupi & Fletcher, 2001)

Teaching the Qualities of Writing: Ideas, Design, Language, Presentation (Portalupi & Fletcher, 2004)

These resources are especially helpful for those just beginning a workshop approach.

Editing

Once revisions to the discovery draft are made, writers move to the editing stage. This is where we teach the rules of our written language and check conventions for capitalization, punctuation, and spelling. Expectations for editing should be appropriate for age and ability. We must be careful not to belabor this part of the process by demanding perfection. For example, asking students to circle five words that don't look right is appropriate versus asking them to correct every misspelled word.

Final Draft

The final draft requires that students rewrite their pieces, incorporating their revisions and editing. The end product will not be perfect, but it will be representative of the best work that they can do at that point in time. If the final draft is going to be published, the teacher acts as final editor and corrects the mistakes before it is published. If it doesn't move to publishing, this draft is placed in the student's writing file. (I use hanging files in a crate.) After students have accumulated a number of writing pieces, they can choose their favorite one to publish.

Publishing

It was a huge relief when I came to the realization that not every piece of writing has to be published. Years ago, before computers, I spent hours typing up stories that my students had written. I wanted them to be excited about writing. This excited them but exhausted me! I've found that, if you let students publish the first piece that they write, they expect to publish all subsequent projects, even though you tell them in the beginning that not all projects will be published. It works well to teach the process up through the final draft several times and then move into publishing. Students can pick a final draft from their writing files that they would like to publish for some purpose.

I've also learned that publishing doesn't necessarily mean a typed product. Publishing is more about audience than format. A published piece is given to someone or displayed for others to read. Pieces can be handwritten, with students using their best penmanship. A cover page can be designed and stapled on top for a finished look.

If your students have limited experience with the writing process, you will need to progress through these stages together for the first several writing projects. After they understand how to move through the process independently, you can give them the freedom to move at their own pace. This is our ultimate goal, to help each writer develop a process that enables him or her to be an independent and effective writer.

7 Using the Writer's Notebook as a Workbench

The best way for students to become skilled is to practice, and the best place to practice is in their own notebooks.

Janet Angelillo (2002, p. 28)

As a farmer, my father had to do lots of building and repairing in order to keep the farm running smoothly. In his shop next to our house was a long workbench with all kinds of tools hanging on the pegboard above it. I remember watching him, his head bent over, intently working on machinery parts, bicycle tires—there wasn't much that he couldn't fix. Sometimes he had to try several tools in order to get things just the way he wanted them.

As a writer, I work like my father did. After jotting my thoughts down on paper, I choose from a variety of crafting tools in order to shape my writing just the way I want it. The tools that I select are not tangible hammers and pliers like my father used. Instead, they are tools of the mind, ready to be applied to a writing task. My writer's notebook becomes the workbench as I try out various tools to strengthen my writing.

Using the Notebook to Plan

Some published authors are intentional about developing a plan for their writing because they want to know the direction in which they are headed. Recently, I had the opportunity to hear Elaine Marie Alphin speak, and she shared how she outlines her books before she begins to write. She wants to know her setting, characters, problems, and resolution before she writes.

Others start writing with an idea in mind and prefer to discover the path along the way. When Avi writes, he doesn't know the ending; that way, both he and the reader can be surprised. His stories unfold as a result of exploration and discovery.

Because writing is such a personal endeavor, we owe it to young writers to expose them to multiple approaches so that they can find what works for them. For certain genres, such as informational text, planning helps organize thoughts before writing. Before I began writing this book, I made an outline so that I could pull my thoughts together and map out a tentative plan.

Graphic Organizers

These are some of the graphic organizers that I've found particularly helpful in working with writers of all ages (see Figure 7.1 for an example).

- Webs and lists help writers think of details to include about their topic.
- Venn diagrams help compare and contrast two things or ideas.
- Pie charts allow writers to narrow their focus by writing about one slice of the pie.
- Story maps are helpful for developing story elements when students are writing fiction.
- Storyboards give an opportunity to sketch (in boxes or on sticky notes) the sequence of events in a story or experience.

Developing Story Elements

A comprehension strategy that we teach readers is to visualize the setting and characters of a story by attending to the author's description. So it makes sense that we ask our students to explore their settings and characters first by sketching or writing about them in their notebooks. When Avi writes a book, he sketches the characters and keeps them propped in front of him so that he gets to know them better.

Another way to become familiar with story characters is to interview them. Elaine Marie Alphin's book, *Creating Characters Kids Will Love* (2000), has a list of questions that writers can ask their characters in order to get to know them in a deeper way. Writers record these questions and fictitious answers in first-person point of view in their notebooks.

Informational Text

The notebook can be used to explore various structures of informational texts, such as comparison/contrast, problem/solution, question/answer, or a combination of structures. When writers learn how to use mentor texts for organizing text, they can plan their writing in their notebooks more effectively.

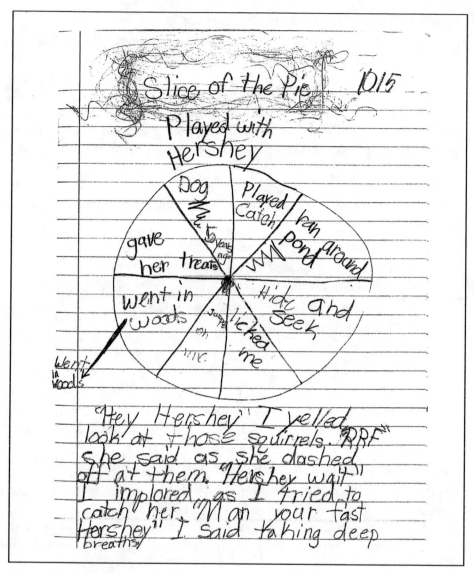

Figure 7.1. Brent's pie chart.

Publishing

When students publish writing projects by making them into books, they can sketch simple pictures in their notebooks before drawing more detailed pictures in the book itself, making sure their sketches match the text. They can also design their book covers and draft their author pages in their notebooks before publishing.

Learning from the Master Craftspeople

One of the best ways that we can help writers become more skillful is to examine the work of those who do it best. By looking closely at the texts of writers whom we want to emulate, we can identify what is effective and give it a try. Use any text—picture books, chapter books, feature articles, teacher and student writing—that demonstrates what you want your students to learn. By exploring a variety of genres together, students will discover that all genres require skilled crafting.

Using Mentor Texts

Mentor texts can be used to take a look at a variety of craft such as the following:

- descriptive writing that uses specific details
- sensory images created by using metaphors or similes
- patterns or repeating text
- point of view and how it strengthens writing
- dialogue and how it moves the story forward
- strong voice
- precise nouns and strong verbs
- leads and endings

Once your students have helped identify and label the craft, it is important to give students an opportunity to try it out in their notebooks.

Writing in a Variety of Genres and Formats

Students enjoy writing in other genres and formats, and the notebook gives them a place to experiment with various types of real-life writing. Don't limit students to the typical school genres such as personal narrative, persuasive, and expository writing. (For poetry, see Chapter 10.)

Letters

Encourage students to write letters to advice columnists, letters of inquiry, letters to state personal opinions, or letters that register complaints. Writers can try several approaches in their notebooks to see which one has the greatest voice and impact. A letter can be taken through the writing process before it is mailed or delivered. Any time that we help young writers find an authentic audience, we are giving

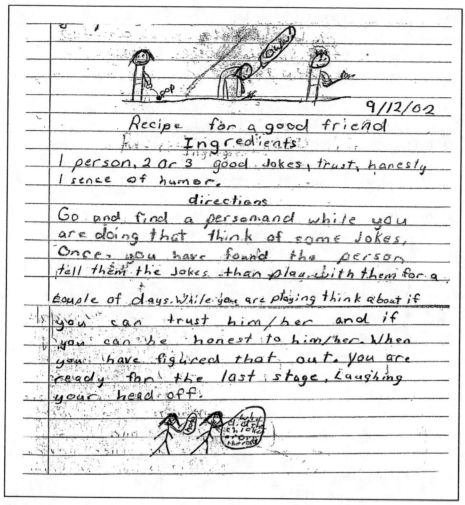

Figure 7.2. Lauren's poem: "How to Make Friends."

them a sense of agency—that writing serves a purpose in life and helps them articulate their thoughts and passions and accomplish their goals.

Recipes

Writing recipes is a fun way to explore various topics. Ingredients and directions can be included for making or doing something out of the ordinary. Figure 7.2 is Lauren's special recipe for making friends. Other possible topics could be the following:

- How to Spend a Summer Day
- How to Survive Fifth Grade
- How to Avoid Homework
- How to Avoid Cleaning Your Room

Speeches

Fifth graders in our district write speeches for the DARE (Drug Abuse Resistance Education) graduation ceremony. Students may run for student council or some other school office. Anytime students have a speech to write, they can plan and develop it in their notebooks.

Interviews

Students can compose questions in their notebooks before conducting interviews and then record the answers during the interview. Often this is done in order to research information about a person or a topic.

Writers also use a number of other formats:

- advertisements
- advice columns
- announcements
- bumper stickers
- captions
- cartoons, jokes, and riddles
- dialogues
- directions
- editorials
- greeting card verses
- instructions
- introductions
- lost and found posters
- memos
- menus
- public notices
- signs
- skits and plays
- slogans
- songs
- speeches
- surveys
- wanted posters

Using the Notebook to Have-a-Go

One of the challenges that I encountered when I began teaching the writing process (described in Chapter 6) occurred after we had moved through the writing process together several times. Once I was able to turn writers loose and give them freedom to move at their own pace, I found that it didn't work to ask students to apply minilessons that didn't fit with the writing stage they were in. (For example, a student who was writing a discovery draft wasn't interested in trying a revision strategy.)

I crossed my fingers and hoped these students would apply the mini-lesson in their writing some time down the road. Most of them didn't.

It took me a while to figure out how to use the writer's notebook to solve this problem. I realized that students could "have-a-go" in their notebooks by writing a new entry, working on a previously written entry, or by using text that I provided and that they glued into their notebooks. By doing this, they demonstrated that they could apply the minilesson and use it effectively in their writing. This exercise was available for revisiting when they did want to try it in a writing project.

The following are some examples of ways to use the notebook to have-a-go.

> Point of view: Choose an entry and change the point of view by writing in first, second, or third person.
>
> Leads: Pick an entry (or use the lead from a writing project) and try some different leads (i.e., question, startling statement, dialogue, setting the scene) and decide which one is most effective.
>
> Dialogue: Select an entry and add dialogue in a couple of strategic places.
>
> Using parenthesis: Choose an entry and step out of the writing to whisper something more to the reader using parenthesis.
>
> Sentence length: Select a topic and write an entry using a variety of long and short sentences.
>
> Sentence structure: Reread an entry to determine the variety of sentence structures.
>
> Rewrite the entry, combining simple sentences, or revise the beginning of sentences, using clauses in order to give variety.

The Gradual Release of Responsibility

In order to set young writers up for success, it's important to release responsibility to them slowly (Pearson and Gallagher, 1983). There's a gradient of support that I keep in mind as I plan my minilessons over a period of time. The amount that writers can handle in one minilesson depends on their writing proficiency and revision expertise.

First of all, in looking at mentor text, my students and I identify and name what the author has done to make the writing so powerful. For example, in this excerpt from *Freedom Summer* (Wiles, 2001), we notice how Deborah Wiles uses comparisons to give readers strong sensory images.

> John Henry's skin is the color of browned butter. He smells like pine needles after a good rain. My skin is the color of pale moths

that dance around the porch light at night. John Henry says I smell like a just washed sock. (p. 12)

After labeling the writer's craft, we use the overhead projector and work together to apply the technique on another piece of writing, usually either my own or a student's writing. Finally, I ask the children to have-a-go in their notebooks, either finding an entry where they can add a comparison or use a comparison in a new entry. My writers are much more successful when I deliberately slow down and allow time for modeling and guided practice.

Once students learn to use their notebooks to plan and try new things as writers, they will find additional ways that their notebooks can support them in other stages of the writing process. No two students will use their workbenches in identical ways. The important thing is that they learn to use them in ways that best support them as crafters of the written word.

8 Creating a Unit of Study for the Writer's Notebook

Lessons about process should come from what people who write say they do, and lessons about how things are written should be matched with real-world text examples.

Katie Wood Ray (2006, p. 181)

When a professional book offers new insight—enough to make lightbulbs go on in my mind—I know that I've discovered a gem. As I began reading Katie Wood Ray's *Study Driven: A Framework for Planning Units of Study in the Writing Workshop* (2006), I immediately had to grab a pencil so that I could underline the important parts. (This book rarely stays on my shelf, because I am either using it or a peer has borrowed it.) Ray's work has enabled me to take great strides as a writer and as a teacher of writers.

Ray challenged me to choose study rather than content as a beginning point in the teaching of writing. I've learned to begin the study of a genre with immersion (reading quality examples) in order to examine the characteristics and craft of the writing. Genre study also considers why writers choose a given genre—what is their purpose? Who is their audience? In other words, genre study connects to the real-life writing that writers do!

I now read with a writer's eye. I automatically think about the genre and what the writer has done well in order to keep me reading. I can't help it. It's as Peter Johnston says in *Choice Words: How Our Language Affects Children's Learning* (2004): "Once we start noticing things, it is difficult not to notice them again" (p. 11). And that's exactly what we want our students to do—to become noticers so that they can grow their writing skills.

Some Important Questions to Ask

When launching a study of the writer's notebook, it's important to consider the questions that Ray suggests when doing a genre study (p. 125). These are the questions:

1. What kinds of topics do writers address with this genre and what kinds of things do they do with these topics?

2. What kinds of work (research, gathering, reflecting, observing, etc.) does it seem like writers of this genre must do in order to produce this kind of writing?

3. How do writers craft this genre so that it is compelling for readers?

The following are the questions that I explore with students when doing a study on the writer's notebook:

1. What is a writer's notebook?

2. What kinds of topics do writers address in their writer's notebooks?

3. What do they do with these topics?

4. What kinds of work does it seem as though writers must do in order to produce notebook writing?

5. How do writers craft notebook writing?

Finding Answers to These Important Questions

These questions have brought us to the following conclusions:

- *What is a writer's notebook?*

  It is some form of a notebook that writers use to collect ideas, observe, try out craft, plan, vent, reflect, sketch, and remember.

- *What kinds of topics do writers address in their writer's notebooks?*

  Writers write about anything and everything! They write about important stuff as well as the small things in life.

- *What kinds of things do they do with these topics?*

  Some writers expand their notebook writing into larger writing projects for some other purpose. Others keep their writing for their own personal satisfaction or growth.

- *What kinds of work does it seem as though notebook writers must do in order to produce this kind of writing?*

  Notebook writers learn to observe carefully—by using all of their senses—and gather interesting information, reflect on experiences, record important life events, and explore creative ideas.

The list grows as the year progresses.

- *How do writers craft notebook writing?*

  This question is so important in a typical genre study. However, when we explore the writer's notebook, we discuss how notebook writing or sketching is primarily for the writer, not for an audience. An entry could be written or molded into any one of a variety of forms or genres, which is when this question becomes relevant.

Great Resources

Resources (in addition to Ray's book) that I have found immensely helpful in this study process are the following:

A Writer's Notebook: Unlocking the Writer within You by Ralph Fletcher

> In this slim paperback, Ralph describes what a notebook is and what it is used for. His audience is young writers, so excerpts can be read to your students. His approach and style make you feel as if he is your writing mentor.

Reflections by Ralph Fletcher

> In Chapter 4, Ralph describes how he uses his writer's notebook.

Five Pages a Day: A Writer's Journey by Peg Kehret

> Peg shares how she recorded in her notebook the conversation of two obnoxious teenage boys and later used that information in her book *Cages*.

Speaking of Journals: Children's Book Writers Talk about Their Diaries, Notebooks, and Sketchbooks by Paula W. Graham

> This book is a "must-have" for your notebook study. In interviews with Paula Graham, twenty-seven children's authors talk about their diaries, notebooks, and sketchbooks. It's an engaging read with a nice variety of authors and of ways in which they use notebooks.

Little by Little: A Writer's Education by Jean Little

> Jean shares how her sixth-grade teacher got her started on notebook writing. Jean was able to use her imagination to move from diary-type entries to imaginative stories.

Nature All Year Long by Claire Walker Leslie

> Sketches and diagrams accompany Leslie's text in this beautiful book that moves through the seasons. It is an appealing example of how naturalists record their observations and information.

Sketching Outdoors in Winter by Jim Arnosky

> Arnosky is a well-known artist, author, and naturalist. This book contains sketches of Arnosky's farm in Vermont, and he includes sketching tips to help readers record their perceptions of the outdoor world.

Amelia's Notebook by Marissa Moss (and additional books in this series)

Max's Logbook by Marissa Moss (and additional books in this series)

All of the books in these series by Moss have great examples and ideas for notebook writing that appeal to young writers. She includes lots of artwork, which makes them visually appealing and entertaining.

The Meet the Author series from Richard C. Owen Publishers, Inc. includes many great biographies that appeal to young readers and writers. Authors share their interests, work habits, and other information that young writers are interested in.

And, of course, don't forget to share examples from your own writer's notebook! I have found a strong correlation between notebook use by students in relation to that of their teachers. When teachers write, kids write.

9 Gathering Language

When I write in my journal, it's like having a meal. It's delicious fragments; it's feasting on the language of the world.

Kim Stafford (cited in Graham, p. 213)

Hey guys, listen to this great language," Courtney called across our fourth-grade classroom one morning during poetry workshop. Aloud she read,

There are purple shadows
And purple veils,
Some ladies purple
Their fingernails.

Hailstones and Halibut Bones (O'Neill, 1961)

Courtney loved the way that Mary O'Neill used the word *purple* as a verb instead of an adjective. Immediately, she walked over to our chart of "Wonderful Words" and added it to the list of language that we loved.

My students didn't always appreciate language in this way. How do we get students to notice language in what they hear and read? It comes by immersing them in language—giving them lots of opportunities to read words, write words, talk about words, and, most important, enjoy words.

Reading Aloud

I love the opportunity to snuggle with my grandson Austin and read a stack of his favorite books. He likes to return to the familiar ones that are filled with rhythm and rhyme—they are fun to listen to. I'll never forget the first time that I read Sandra Boynton's book *Blue Hat, Green Hat* (1984) to him when he was six months old. Each time I read the word *oops*, he broke out in giggles. My husband and I were in tears by the end of the book from laughing at his joyful response. This book is still one of his many favorites that we enjoy together.

Someday soon, my grandson will write with these ears that have been tuned into language since he was born, perhaps even before. His verbal vocabulary is growing by leaps and bounds as he soaks up and repeats the language used by those around him. Being read to is important for writers of all ages, as Mem Fox shares in her book about her life:

Even in my forties I have benefited as a writer directly from hearing writing read aloud. The music, the word choice, the feelings, the flow of structure, the new ideas, the fresh thoughts—all these and more are banked into my writing checking account whenever I am fortunate enough to be read to. (1993, p. 70)

Students' word banks need be filled with a treasury of rich words. One way to make deposits is to select carefully read-alouds that are beautifully written. As parents, grandparents, and teachers, we have so many wonderful picture books available today. There are many important reasons to read picture books to intermediate students—with exposure to rich language being only one of them.

The following are excerpts from some of my favorite read-alouds:

Freedom Summer by Deborah Wiles

"John Henry's skin is the color of browned butter. He smells like pine needles after a good rain. My skin is the color of pale moths that dance around the porch light at night. John Henry says I smell like a just-washed sock" (p. 7). (Deborah's words make me feel better about my pale complexion!)

Come On, Rain! by Karen Hesse

"It streams through our hair and down our backs. It freckles our feet, glazes our toes. We turn in circles, glistening in our rain skin. Our mouths wide, we gulp down rain" (p. 18).

Sister Anne's Hands by Maribeth Lorbiecki

"When she reached out to touch my cheek, I dodged her hand as if it were hot. It was puppy brown with white lacy moons for nails. And palm side up, it was pink with dark lines. A light pretty pink like an evening dress for Barbie" (p. 7).

I was browsing a *Cricket* magazine the other day and came across a page with favorite first sentences that young readers had contributed. Kids had emailed or mailed the first sentences, filled with wonderful language, of books that they had read. What a great idea on the editor's part and a great resource to share with students.

Reading poetry aloud is another powerful way to tune students into language. I love the way that Bobbi Katz describes the lure of words: "I write poetry for the same reason I read it: the sound of words, their taste on my tongue, is irresistible. Words are the apple pie in my pantry that draws me out of my warm bed and sends me shuffling down the dark hall in the middle of the night" (cited in Heard, 1990, p. 82).

So take time to browse picture books and poetry books to find language that you love. Read aloud beautiful language everyday to your students and share why you selected it. Katie Wood Ray advises us to "Look for language that is stunning, rereadable, readaloudable" (Ray, 1999, p. 79). I might add, look for language that is memorable. Read it aloud again and again—either to, by, or with your students. Immerse them so that they have the opportunity to develop an ear for language and to listen like writers.

Recording Language

In *Sahara Special* (Codell, 2003), Sahara's fifth-grade teacher encourages her to write by giving her tips when she responds in Sahara's journal. One day she wrote to Sahara, "If you hear a good word that belongs to someone else, write it down somewhere so it belongs to you, too" (p. 85).

The writer's notebook is the perfect place to collect language that is memorable, fun, or amazing. I encourage writers to tab a section in the back of their notebooks so that they have a place to record words and phrases that they love and want to remember. Together we think of ideas for a title for this page such as Amazing Words, Wonderful Words, Words I Love, or something similar.

I introduce this idea of collecting words by saying something like this: "Do you have words that you like the sound of or love to say? Maybe you like how the syllables roll off your tongue or you enjoy the musical quality of their sounds. Or you love the image that they create in your mind." I prime writers by sharing some of the favorite words from my list, such as *smithereens* and *discombobulated*. I also ask them to think about people they know who use (or have used) a special word frequently.

When I was young, my mother used to call the creative bits of paper that I left behind after cutting with scissors *snipples*. I loved the sound of that word, even though it was a synonym for a mess! Later, in seventh grade, I had a math teacher who used the word *facetious* on a daily basis it seemed. It took me a while to figure out the meaning of the word, but I liked the way it sounded.

I've just added another great word to my list, which is *twidderpated*. A teacher introduced me to it; she learned it from her grandmother. It means the kind of excitement that gives you butterflies in your stomach—like puppy love. Every teacher listening to Lisa share her favorite word quickly turned to the word sections in their notebooks and jotted it down.

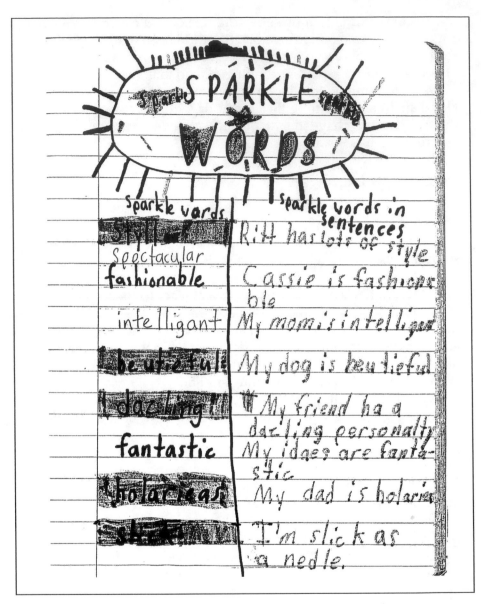

Figure 9.1. Charlotte's sparkle words.

We've enjoyed using *twitterpated* in conversation with each other and have begun to make it our own.

Figures 9.1 and 9.2 reveal the interest that Charlotte, as a third grader, has in words. Not only has she written words in her notebook,

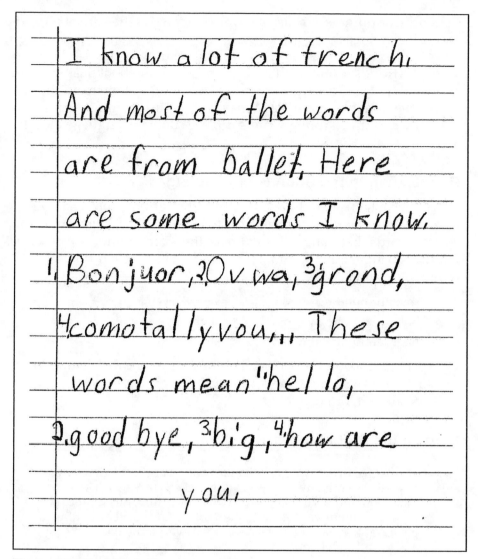

Figure 9.2. Charlotte's French words.

she has also recorded the French words that she's been exposed to in her ballet lessons.

It requires nudging, reminding, and lots of sharing to get young writers in the habit of using their notebooks to record intriguing language. Sticky notes can be used to jot down words that students encounter during reading to transfer to their notebook later on. Paragraphs, sentences, or phrases can also be copied; often it is the sum of all of the words that creates the beauty of the passage. Words can be gleaned from newspapers, magazines, chapter books, poems, greeting cards, or any kind of writing. A phrase that I copied in my notebook last fall came from a journalist's description of the glorious fall colors in our town: "a vegetative rainbow." Someday I may want to use a similar description in my own writing. Young writers can also borrow language that they love, to use in their own writing.

Responding to the Sounds of Language

Fabrics have texture, but have you ever thought of words having texture? Georgia Heard (*Awakening the Heart*, 1999, p. 90) suggests writing a list of words that match the texture of the word-sound. She describes words as being smooth, bumpy, or hard. When I tried this activity, I wrote the following:

smooth sounding words	swim, love
bumpy sounding words	radical, persnickety
hard sounding words	stop, crack

Georgia also encourages us to hear words as musical instruments and to illustrate the sounds of words (not their meanings) by drawing curved, straight, or jagged lines.

Finding the Right Words

> Sometimes I've spent weeks looking for precisely the right word. It's like having a tiny marble in your pocket; you can feel it. Sometimes you find a word and say, "No, I don't think this is precisely it." Then you discard it, and take another and another until you get it right. What I like to stress above everything else is the joy and sounds of language.
>
> Eve Merriam (cited in Cullinan, 1996, p. 66)

We need to teach our young writers how to play with language, try it one way, try it another way. Read it aloud—what words give it rhythm? What words are crisp and emphatic? We can join hands with our budding writers and help them feel that tiny marble fitting perfectly in the palms of their hands.

10 Integrating Poetry

My journal is stuffed with notes that I've taken at different places. I carry index cards in my wallet for that purpose. Then I transpose my observations into my journal. Some of the ideas I develop: I'll recreate the scene or make comments about it; others I just transfer. It may take years before notes end up in a poem, if at all.

Sara Holbrook (cited in Graham, 1999, p. 149)

I begin the year by immersing students in poetry of all kinds. We spend time sitting on the floor, browsing baskets of poetry books, reading poems to each other, feasting on the banquet of words. After we've had ample time to savor them, we come together and chart all of the topics of the poems that we've read. It doesn't take long for the list to fill the entire chart. Nor does it take long for students to realize that poems can be written about anything—from drinking fountains to dragons. Everything collected between the covers of a notebook holds the potential for a poem if the writer feels the emotion or desire to create one.

My unfortunate observation of two fast-food employees arguing and disrupting my peaceful lunch made me disgusted enough to write down my observations and feelings. I thought a lot about the power of words and eventually turned my notes into a poem . The format lent itself to a poem for two voices.

Words, Words, Words

agreement

ARGUMENT

compliment

CRITICISM

soothing

IRRITATING

humorous

ANGRY

eloquent

CRUDE

helpful

HURTFUL

A gift
  or

OR
A CURSE

words,	WORDS,
words,	WORDS,
words.	WORDS!

I've written poems about my grandmother's quilt (triggered by a picture in my notebook), poems for family celebrations, gifts of poetry for friends, and more. Each poem originated in my notebook, and I show students how my seeds turned into poems.

Writing Poetry

One of the most liberating things that young writers can learn about poetry is that it doesn't have to rhyme. At the beginning of the year, I give my students a poetry survey—to get a feel for their thoughts and attitudes. I never fail to be surprised at the number of students (of all ages) who define poetry as rhyming words. As I explore important aspects of poetry—such as emotion, sparse use of words, use of white space, rhythm, creation of images, and more—with students, they learn how free verse is an easier way to say what is thought, seen, and felt. (We've probably all cringed at the words that young writers have used in desperation, just so that they could get their poems to rhyme!)

Using Format as a Model for Writing Poems

Even with free verse, it is difficult for some young writers to feel comfortable composing poetry. There are ways to scaffold them by using the format of a poem as a model. List poems are a fun and easy way to get started. They can be composed with one-word lines, phrases, or sentences. Doug Florian is a master of the list poem as demonstrated in his seasonal poetry books: *Summersaults* (2002), *Winter Eyes* (1999), and *Handsprings* (2006). His books will give your students a variety of examples for list poems. Using the list format, Lauren wrote a poem in her notebook about playing a basketball game (see Figure 10.1). After reading and spending time appreciating and discussing George Ella Lyon's poem *Where I'm From*, Lizbeth wrote the poem "I Am From" in sixth grade (see Figure 10.2).

Brainstorm additional ideas for list poems with your students such as the following:

- The sound of a new baby brother or sister
- Things that annoy me
- My grandmother's house
- Lies that I've told
- When I'm alone, I . . .

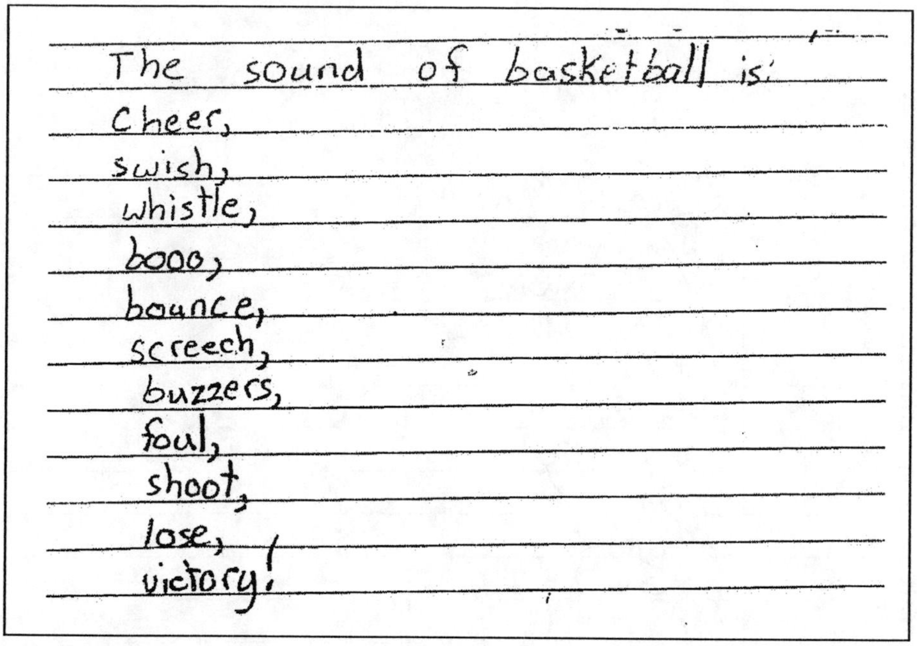

The sound of basketball is:
cheer,
swish,
whistle,
booo,
bounce,
screech,
buzzers,
foul,
shoot,
lose,
victory!

Figure 10.1. Lauren's list poem.

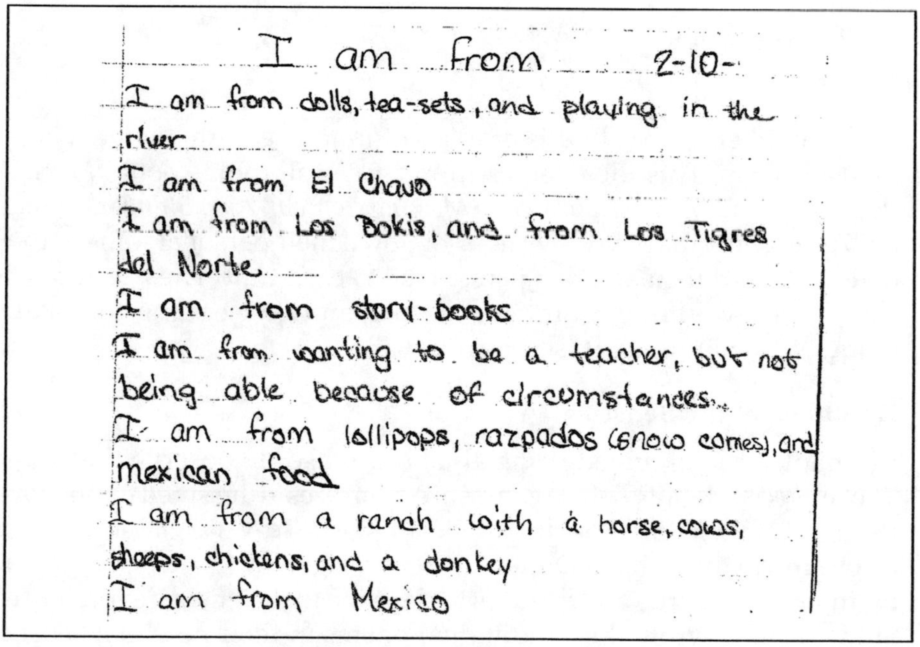

I am from   2-10-
I am from dolls, tea-sets, and playing in the
river.
I am from El Chavo
I am from Los Bokis, and from Los Tigres
del Norte
I am from story-books
I am from wanting to be a teacher, but not
being able because of circumstances.
I am from lollipops, razpados (snow cones), and
mexican food
I am from a ranch with a horse, cows,
sheeps, chickens, and a donkey
I am from Mexico

Figure 10.2. Lizbeth's poem: "I Am From."

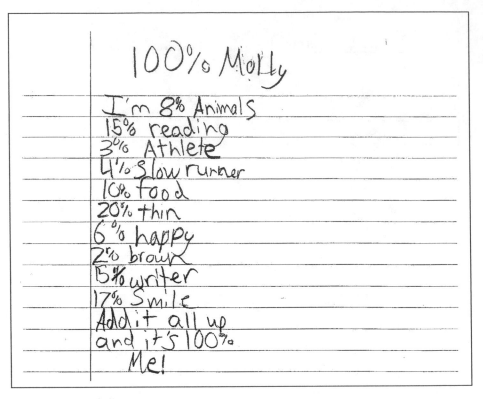

Figure 10.3. Molly's percentage poem.

Another format that is easy and fun to use with students is the "100% poem." This idea comes from Sara Holbrook's book, *Practical Poetry: A Nonstandard Approach to Meeting Content-Area Standards* (2005, pp. 76–79). First, have your writers jot down their personal traits in their notebooks and then assign a percentage to each trait. The poem can be completed by adding an interesting beginning or ending to make it unique to the individual (see Figure 10.3).

Don't Forget the Senses

In Chapter 4, I discussed using all of our senses to observe the world. Those precise details help create sensory images—the smell of popcorn, the howl of the wind. Fourth graders in Krista Troyer's classroom took a field trip to the Indiana Dunes. On returning, they formed groups and brainstormed words and phrases to describe their sensory experiences. Students then wrote their individual poems in their notebooks, using

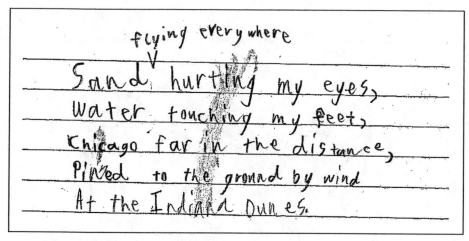

flying everywhere

Sand hurting my eyes,
Water touching my feet,
Chicago far in the distance,
Pined to the ground by wind
At the Indiana Dunes.

Figure 10.4. Ethan's poem about the Indiana Dunes.

words and phrases generated on the sensory charts. See Figure 10.4 for the poem Ethan wrote in his notebook.

Finding Ideas for Poems

Another challenge for young poets can be finding topics that they want to invest some energy in. In her book *Awakening the Heart: Exploring Poetry in Elementary and Middle School* (1999), Georgia Heard describes her work using heart maps with children. She feels it is the "poet's job to know the interior of his or her heart" (p. 109). In order to discover what matters to them, students draw representations of their hearts in their notebooks and show what is important to them. In Figure 10.5, you can see what Taylor included in his heart map.

Heard says, "The point of heart mapping is not necessarily to write poems but to access the feelings, memories, and reflections that are the source of poetry: to sharpen our inner vision. Later, as an extension, I might ask students to select one part of their heart maps that they could explore in more detail, write a reflection from, and then write a poem" (p. 111). Stephany, a seventh grader, has a whole list of ideas in her notebook for when she finds herself in need of ideas for poetry (see Figure 10.6).

Finding Words

Once a topic is chosen, an activity that helps young poets get words on paper is "wordstorming." In Margriet Ruurs's book *The Power of Poems:*

Figure 10.5. Taylor's heart map.

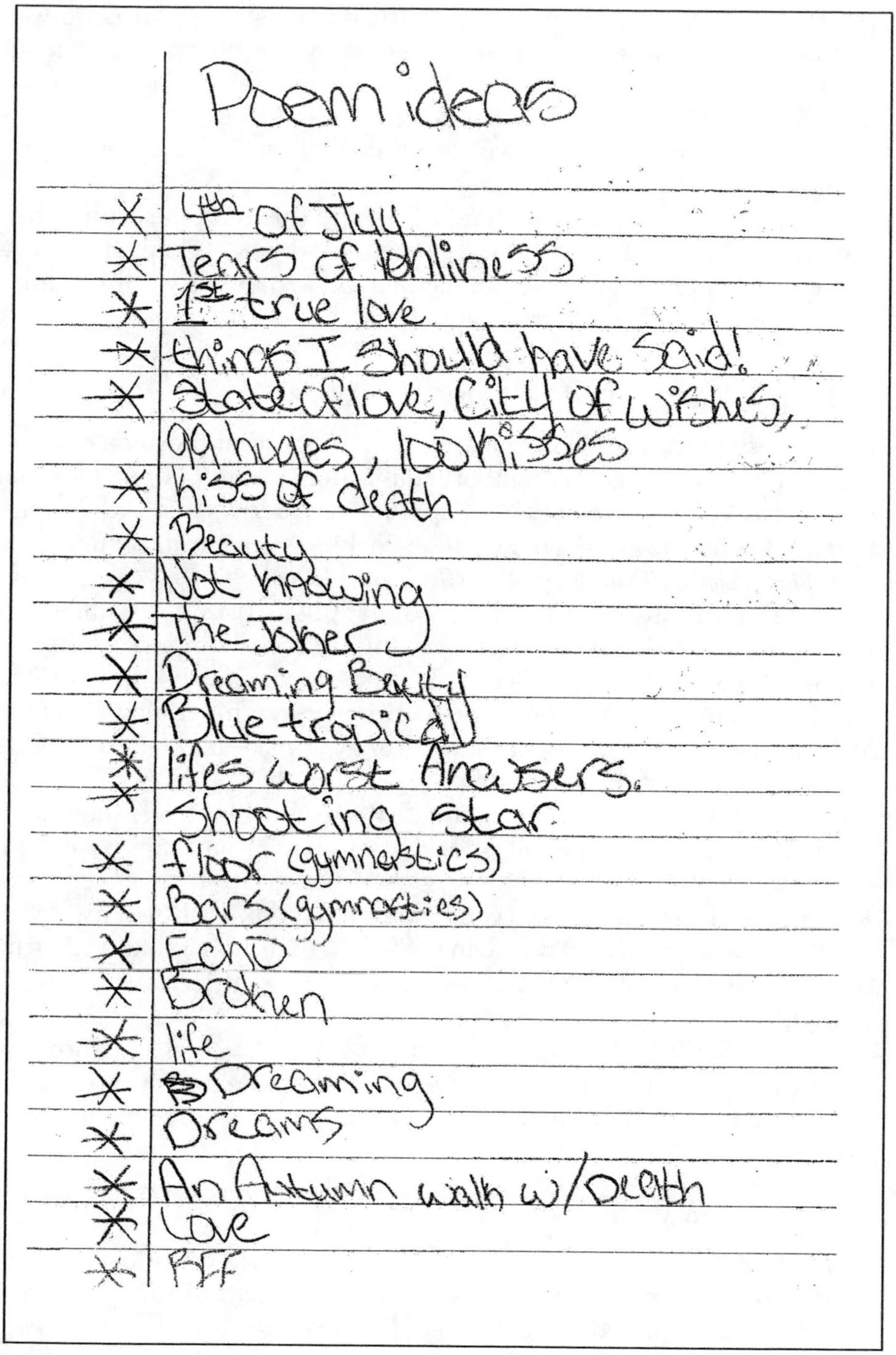

Poem ideas

* 4th of July
* Tears of lonliness
* 1st true love
* things I should have said!
* State of love, City of wishes,
  99 huges, 100 kisses
* kiss of death
* Beauty
* Not knowing
* The Joker
* Dreaming Beauty
* Blue tropical
* lifes worst Answers
  Shooting star
* floor (gymnastics)
* Bars (gymnastics)
* Echo
* Broken
* life
* Dreaming
* Dreams
* An Autumn walk w/Death
* Love
* BFF

Figure 10.6. Stephany's list of ideas for poems.

Teaching the Joy of Writing Poetry (2001, p. 31), she explains how to wordstorm with your students. Write a word on the board and jot down all of the descriptive words that the students contribute. Then ask questions to generate more words to add to the list. Once the board is covered and students run out of words, invite them to write a poem using some of the words on the board.

When students have learned how to do this with the group, they can wordstorm their own topics in their notebooks when they write poetry. This activity not only opens their eyes to the possibilities for a poem, it also increases their vocabularies.

Writing in Response to Poetry

It is important that we help children find poems that they can connect to their everyday lives. Valerie Worth has a great book titled, *All the Small Poems and Fourteen More* (1994). I appreciate Valerie's everyday topics that are familiar to children. Her titles include such common things as *Sun, Dog, Pebbles, Toad, Pumpkin, Clock,* and *Door.*

I've given my students a copy of her poem *Shoes* as a catalyst for writing a notebook entry. I share the story of my favorite black patent leather shoes that turned into my play shoes once they became scuffed and worn. I loved those shoes, each with a little white daisy attached, so I was saddened to discover that one of the daisies had fallen off. One summer morning when I was helping my mother butcher chickens, I accidentally sliced open the bag inside the gizzard I was cleaning and, to my surprise, the daisy fell out! That chicken apparently thought it was a delectable treat when she happened across it in the chicken yard.

When I use a poem as a catalyst for notebook writing, I give each child a small copy of it so they can paste it in their notebooks and write beside it. They enjoy having a copy and may want to return to it for other ideas.

Another way to respond to poetry is to ask writers to borrow a line from a poem to write from. They write that line in their notebooks and respond with thoughts, questions, connections—whatever comes to mind.

Responding to Meaning

What does this poem mean or say to you? This is a question that students can answer honestly in their notebooks without fear of being wrong or embarrassed. Discussion of possible interpretations can help with this process as you begin. Then turn it over to your writers to write their own thoughts in their notebooks.

You can also give your students two poems to compare in their notebooks. What are the similarities? How do they differ? You can compare the structures, moods, content, or other features of the poems. You will want to do this with your students several times before asking them to do it independently. It's not right answers that we're looking for, but rather depth of analysis and thought. We want to encourage thinking, not teach the poem.

Collecting Poems

One of my favorite ways to use my writer's notebook is to collect poems that I love. I copy the poems that inspire me, have beautiful language, or give me ideas for my own poetry. When you encourage your students to do this, make sure they understand that they must give the author credit so someone doesn't mistake it for their own poem. (This happened to one teacher who thought a poem was brilliant until she found out her student had copied it and forgotten to write down the author's name.)

Collecting Information about Poets

I encourage my students to find at least one poet during the course of the year whose poems they appreciate and love. Once they discover these poets, they can research them—to discover writing habits, where they get their ideas, and other interesting information about their personal life. These notes are recorded in the writer's notebook and shared with the entire class so that everyone can benefit from the research and become more familiar with a variety of poets.

With the examples that I have shared, you can see how notebooks offer possibilities for incorporating poetry in practical ways. I know that you and your students will be able to think of many more exciting and productive ways to make poetry an integral part of this journey.

11 Engaging Boys in Notebook Writing

Literacy too often seems unappealing and inactive to boys. It gets in the way of the need to move, to talk, to play, to live in and with one's body . . . as many boys claim, when they are writing these adventures, they feel themselves physically inside the stories. Rather than denying the physical needs of boys, writing can employ that energy—if we keep the space open for their play.

Thomas Newkirk (2002, p. 178)

A few weeks ago, I visited a teacher's sixth-grade classroom and was introduced to a new book: *Diary of a Wimpy Kid* by Jeff Kinney (2007). As I read the first two pages, I began to understand why Jennie's students, especially her boys, were loving it as a read-aloud. It begins like this:

SEPTEMBER
Tuesday
     First of all, let me get something straight: This is a JOURNAL, not a diary. I know what it says on the cover, but when Mom went out to buy this thing I SPECIFICALLY told her to get one that didn't say "diary" on it.
     Great. All I need is for some jerk to catch me carrying this book around and get the wrong idea. The other thing I want to clear up right away is that this was MOM's idea, not mine.
     But if she thinks I'm going to write down my "feelings" in here or whatever, she's crazy. So just don't expect me to be all "Dear Diary" this and "Dear Diary" that.
     The only reason I agreed to do this at all is because I figure later on when I'm rich and famous, I'll have better things to do than answer people's stupid questions all day long. So this book is gonna come in handy.
     Like I said, I'll be famous one day, but for now I'm stuck in middle school with a bunch of morons. (pp. 1–2)

Not only is this book written in the authentic voice of a sixth-grade boy, it includes humorous cartoons that enhance the text on nearly every page. In a clever way, Kinney combines an appealing format and voice with a topic that may not be high on some boys' lists of things to do.

How do we help boys flourish as writers? How do we help them see that notebook writing is not just for girls or "sissies"? In his keynote address (at the 7th Annual Summer Literacy Institute of the Purdue Literacy Network Project , July, 2007) entitled "Creating Boy-Friendly Writing Classrooms," Ralph Fletcher gives three reasons why boys aren't flourishing as writers in classrooms:

1. Topic choice: Not enough freedom is given to write about what boys want to write about.

2. Violence: Boys want to write about things that are uncomfortable—edgy. As teachers, we have to develop a taste or, at least, an understanding of boy writing.

3. Humor: Adolescent male humor is typically not enjoyed or appreciated by most teachers.

Topic Choice

As discussed earlier in this book, topic choice is important for all writers, but it is especially important for boys. Freedom of topic choice doesn't mean that students can't be guided with some parameters, but there should be lots of opportunity to choose what to write about. In surveying young writers' attitudes and habits toward the writer's notebooks, I noted a big difference in what girls and boys like to write about. These are the answers that fifth- and sixth-grade boys gave to the question: What are your favorite topics to write about?

fantasy or science fiction "novels"

scary and funny stories

animals and fantasy

sports, games

make-believe stories

exaggerating stupidity and humorous things

cars and wars

war, comedy, and fantasy

cheap, corny, humorous stories

stories

poems

humor

riddles

mysteries, action, and adventure

horror and comedy

Figure 11.1. Sam's drawing.

Violence

With freedom of choice comes the issue of violence. Recently, my officemate handed me two drawings that her own children had presented to her. Her comment was, "Same parents, same environment, same values, look at the difference." Their pictures are shown in Figure 11.1 and Figure 11.2.

Figure 11.2. Molly's drawing.

Already, six-year-old Sam is showing some potentially violent events in his storytelling. A man in a parachute drops down amidst an army tank that is firing on a giant walking turtle who is approaching a skyscraper. The picture is waiting to explode! (I must add that Sam is a strong first-grade reader and writer and is a sensitive, delightful boy.) In contrast, his ten-year-old sister Molly, drew a pastoral scene filled with blue sky, fluffy clouds, and a contented horse.

As a teacher, which artist would you encourage? Which one would you discourage? A few years ago, I would have been inclined to steer Sam away from drawing and writing such stories for fear that they would encourage violent behavior. However, my thinking has changed since reading two books: *Misreading Masculinity: Boys, Literacy, and Popular Culture* by Thomas Newkirk (2002) and *Boy Writers: Reclaiming Their Voices* by Ralph Fletcher (2006a). Both are thought-provoking books for teachers and parents. The authors make readers take pause and consider what motivates and interests males, as well as challenge us to accept some writing that previously may have been taboo. Newkirk addresses how writing could be a dangerous, supervised sport. Are we willing to go out on a limb to coach this dangerous sport?

Does that mean that we have to accept violence of any nature in their writings? Newkirk says, "Any categorical banning of violence would effectively preclude their attempting their favorite genres, removing one of the few motivations boys have to attempt writing" (p. 175). However, he also says that boys recognize some reasonable limits, and he recommends discussing violence in the media and the effects it has on us with our students. Also, writing that causes teachers or classmates to feel threatened or belittled is inappropriate. The line is not easily drawn, but we can hope to discuss the issue with those who cross that line without having to penalize them.

Humor

If you've ever been around adolescent boys, you know that bodily functions, disgusting noises, sarcasm, and other similar behaviors crack them up. (I grew up with five brothers, raised two sons, have three grandsons, a husband, and a male dog!) As a parent, tolerance and humor got me through the adolescent stage of my sons' lives. As a teacher, I've learned to accept some of this from boy writers as well. Fletcher recommends that we take boys' humor seriously and look for the intelligence behind it. We should seek to understand their humor and "make a distinction between what is destructive and what is merely irreverent" (*Boy Writers*, p. 68).

Sketching

Fletcher promotes the "radical idea" that upper-grade boys benefit from drawing as a part of the composing process: "Unfortunately, teachers in most classrooms don't see drawing as an activity with much intrinsic value during writing time. Instead, drawing is viewed warily as something kids get away with, like chewing gum or listening to an iPod on the sly . . . Perhaps we consider it time off-task or feel nervous that drawing is a distraction that pulls kids away from real writing" (*Boy Writers*, pp. 121–122,128).

Nikolai, an English language learner, used sketches to record information about weather (his passion). Figure 11.3 is one of many pages filled with drawings that include details about tornadoes, temperature in different countries, and more.

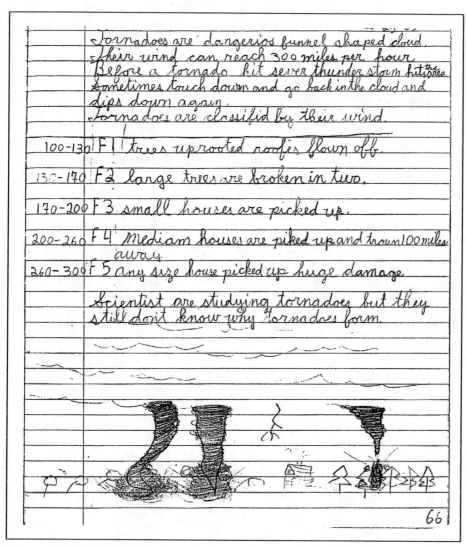

Figure 11.3. Nikolai's sketch.

Newkirk (*Misreading Masculinity*, 2002) addresses the changing definition of the word *text*. In the world of technology, we continually find new and engaging ways of communicating through digital stories, streaming videos, and other venues.

Linda Rief includes a chapter in *Vision and Voice: Extending the Literacy Spectrum* (1998) that helps teachers understand why sketching in notebooks is important and how to help students be successful. She also addresses cartooning, which is a popular genre for many boys.

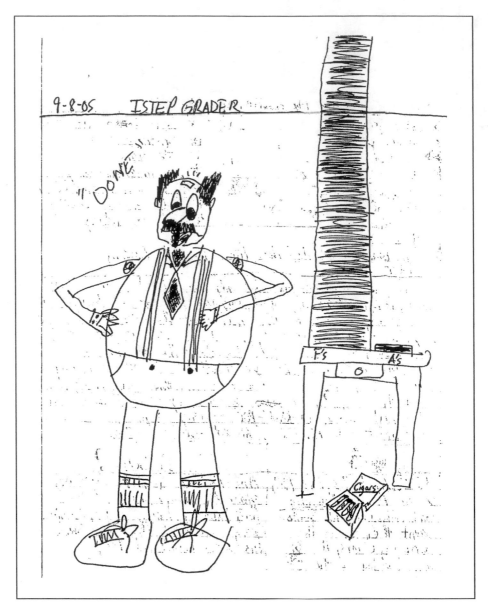

Figure 11.4. Nicolas's cartoon.

Linda's information—as well as discussions on various sites on the web (search under "cartooning")—can help you with a study of comics and cartooning. See Figure 11.4 for the perceptions that eighth grader Nicolas has of that suspect person who grades the standardized tests in our state.

Max's Logbook by Marissa Moss is a great mentor text to use for sketching. Max's drawings are a great example of how humor and text can create an interesting read.

Kinds of Writing That Appeal to Boys

As we plan the genres to study throughout the year, we need to be intentional about including some that appeal to boys. Look at your writers. Does drawing energize them? Do you have a room full of sports fanatics? Are they into fantasy, scary stories? What excites and interests your male students?

My sons, who were sports enthusiasts, were always attempting to write about sports when they were young. They would have loved learning about sports writing. I recently discovered a great resource for this genre written by Steve Craig: *Sports Writing: A Beginner's Guide* (2002). Much of what Craig covers in his book is pertinent for any genre of writing. He includes information on conducting interviews and writing feature stories, as well as an explanation of what his job requires.

The writer's notebook can be a workbench for sports writing and for writing in every other genre: gathering information, recording observations, planning the writing, practicing the craft—all of this can be done in the pages of a notebook.

I challenge you to become more open-minded in regard to the male voices in your classrooms and allow them to speak through sketching and writing. Fletcher's and Newkirk's books go into much more depth on this issue and help you think through why we need to be more accepting and deliberate. I also encourage you to consider including more "boy-friendly" genres in your yearlong writing curriculum. Do you need to include a unit on fantasy, sports writing, or scary stories? Step outside your comfort zone and see how your boy writers respond.

12 Using the Notebook Across the Curriculum

Naturally, each classroom has to find its own possibilities for writer's note-
books and then must continually outgrow that list, not be limited to it.

Randy Bomer (1995, p. 53)

Recently, I was firming up plans to visit one of the fourth-grade teachers who is a member of my training class. Barb invited me to arrive early so that I could listen to a guest author speak to the students. Much to my surprise and delight, this author turned out to be Elaine Marie Alphin, who was my writing instructor when I took the Institute of Children's Literature correspondence writing course. I never imagined that one day I would get to meet her in person. I enjoyed hearing about her writing experiences and writing habits. I scribbled notes in my writer's notebook as I tried to absorb everything that she shared. Meeting and talking with her in person after the presentation will always be one of the highlights of my writing career. She taught me so much, in such a gentle way, and I will always be grateful to her for nurturing me at a time when I had little expertise or confidence as a writer.

When I had a few minutes, I reflected on this chance encounter (if anything happens by chance) and jotted down my thoughts and feelings beside Elaine's picture in my notebook. I pondered the purpose of this stroke of luck and came to the conclusion that her encouraging words gave me renewed energy to finish this book. (A writer's energy sometimes fizzles toward the end of a project!)

As Barb and I discussed her plans for writer's workshop that day, she decided that she wanted to give students an opportunity to reflect in their notebooks. She gave each student a copy of Elaine's picture and asked them to record what they had learned from her or wanted to remember. In Figure 12.1, read Spencer's entry to catch a glimpse of what he will remember from Elaine's visit.

Teachers like Barb learn to recognize opportunities like this and use the writer's notebook in various ways. Once you get in the habit of looking for possibilities, you can broaden your students' use of notebooks in a variety of ways and in various content areas.

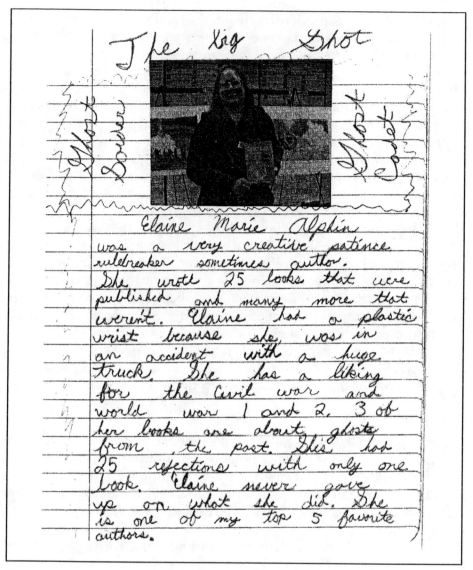

The Keg Shot

Elaine Marie Alphin
was a very creative satince
rulebreaker sometimes auttor.
She wrote 25 books that were
published and many more that
weren't. Elaine had a plastic
wrist because she was in
an accident with a huge
truck. She has a liking
for the Civil war and
world war 1 and 2. 3 of
her books are about ghosts
from the past. She had
25 rejections with only one
book. Elaine never gave
up on what she did. She
is one of my top 5 favorite
authors.

Figure 12.1. Spencer's reflection.

Social Studies and Science

Grade levels have different standards for social studies curricula. Fourth graders typically study state history and fifth graders learn about U.S. history. Within these parameters, the notebook can be a workbench for investigating a person, place, or event that is connected to these standards.

For example, fourth graders can begin the inquiry process by making a list of people, places, and events in their state that interest them. Once they narrow their topic, they can browse resources and jot down wonderings or questions regarding their topic. Then they can research the topic in a variety of ways and take notes in their notebooks. (It's helpful to brainstorm with your class the kinds of questions to ask or to allow students to browse through books on the topics in order to stimulate questions.)

One way to do primary research is through interviews. Writing down questions in the notebook ahead of time helps students focus on what they want to learn and guides their conversation. Recording the answers to the questions ensures that they have accurate information.

Nothing can replace the real-life experiences that we can offer our students. Encourage your students to write and sketch in their notebooks on field trips or to reflect afterward to help them express what they thought was important or intriguing. Some teachers worry about notebooks getting lost or destroyed. If this becomes a problem, students can write on a separate sheet of paper and glue it into their notebooks on returning to the classroom.

Brent expresses his thoughts regarding a trip he and his class took to Sauder Village in Ohio (see Figure 12.2). Assemblies and guest speakers also provide opportunities for reflection.

State Standards

Examine your state standards for the content areas to see where you could incorporate the writer's notebook. For example, Standard 5.1.10 for fifth grade (Indiana Department of Education, 2001) says: "Examine the causes and consequences of the establishment of slavery and describe how slavery became an issue to divide the Northern and Southern colonies."

One student responded to her reading of the Addy series (American Girls Collection by Connie Porter) and wrote, "I think it was mean for the South to buy and sell slaves. I understand now why the whites needed slaves. It was because they needed tobacco plants wormed and crops and cotton picked, but why couldn't they do it? I'm glad that the North won or else I would be a slave!"

A science standard, Standard 4.4.9, for fourth grade (Indiana Department of Education, 2000) says: "Explain that food provides energy and materials for growth and repair of body parts. Recognize that vitamins and minerals, present in small amounts of food, are essential to keep everything working well." When studying nutrition, students can

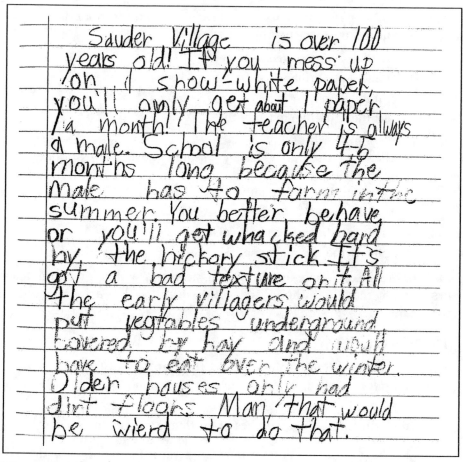

Figure 12.2. Brent's field trip reflection.

list the foods that they eat and possibly record label information in order to examine their diets for essential nutrients.

Responding to Media

Teachers can gain insight and extend understanding when students use their notebooks to jot down thoughts and reactions in response to videos during social studies and science class. I remember daydreaming through too many 16-millimeter reel-to-reel movies in school many years ago. If I had been given some thought-provoking questions to reflect on in writing or important concepts to discuss afterward, I would have been challenged to think more deeply and would have been more engaged.

Over the past few years, various classes in our school district have had the following opportunities:

- Attend a Civil War reenactment.
- Attend a performance of *The Nutcracker Suite*.
- Visit the local courthouse.
- Visit the aquarium in Chicago.
- Visit the local hospital.
- Attend an assembly given by a search and rescue team (and their dogs).
- Participate in a rocket launch.
- Attend an outdoor camp for three days.
- Listen to authors and poets speak.
- Listen to the city mayor speak.

Each of these experiences could be enhanced by notebook writing; teachers learn to recognize the various opportunities that arise throughout the year.

The Two Faces of Writing

Randy and Katherine Bomer discuss the two faces of writing in *For a Better World: Reading and Writing for Social Action* (2001):

> One face is directed outward toward others—it's the writing you do for readers. The other face of writing is the one that in some way is turned inward to the writer, the writing that is a tool for thinking rather than communicating. This is the writing you do to plan your life and activity, to think through your responses to your world, to claim your position, to craft the self you want to be. (p. 111)

In Figure 12.3, a seventh grader's inward face is revealed in her reflection on equality.

Katie Wood Ray (1999) encourages us to develop our outward face: "'Having our say' is such a good, good reason to write" (p. 100). Who among us doesn't want our voice to be heard? Who doesn't have strong feelings and opinions about the things that we would like to change in our lives and in our world?

Allowing students to respond to editorials, current events, political cartoons, assemblies, and guest speakers gives them an opportunity to express their thoughts and opinions. The thinking that students record in their notebooks can logically lead to writing for an audience. Figure 12.4 is an example of a response that a sixth grader wrote about a car-

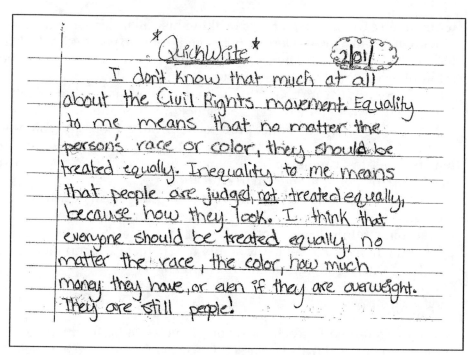

Figure 12.3. Lauren's quick write on equality.

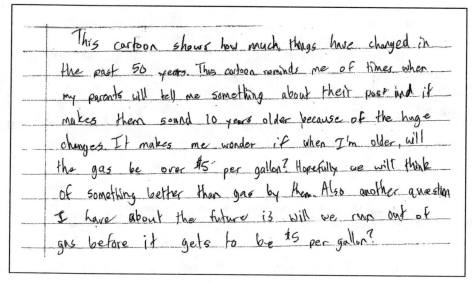

Figure 12.4. Warren's thoughts provoked by a cartoon.

toon. In the cartoon, a father was walking his son to school and telling him how he had to walk a long way through snow to get to school when he was his son's age. The son responded with a comment on the affordability of gas being a problem in his father's day, too.

Currently, we are going through an election year in our country. I am jotting down in my writer's notebook my thoughts and reactions to the candidates and the entire process. Political cartoons and columns are pasted in, with responses written on the side. I have already written one letter to a candidate (to be sent if this person becomes our next president), pleading for reform in education.

My inner face is very naturally transitioning to an outward face. Notebook entries can be catalysts for letters to parents, editors, teachers, administrators, legislators, and other audiences. Students are empowered when they develop the ability to articulate their opinions and beliefs in order to become agents of change.

Integrating the Arts

If you are required to teach music or art, you can easily integrate the writer's notebook into these classes. If you are fortunate to have teachers who teach the arts, I encourage you to collaborate with them so that they learn how to integrate notebook writing into their classes.

In art class, students can record their thoughts and interpretations regarding paintings, style, or use of color. When studying a particular artist, students can use their notebook to record important information or to reflect on something special about the artist.

Clay or play dough can be used for molding shapes, and young sculptors can then write about their creations after they are finished. This activity lends itself to creative stories written about the sculptured pieces.

Writers can respond to music selections by sketching or writing what they are thinking about as they listen to the music.

What does the song or music remind you of?

How does it make you feel?

How do the lyrics impact you? What is the message?

When sketching to music, what does it cause you to draw: wavy lines, circles, jagged lines?

When I did this exercise with teachers, we listened to tropical music. Sandy was taken back in time to a cruise, and by writing in her notebook she was able to relive some of the great things she had experienced.

Just as in art class, students can record important information learned about music, composers, or musicians. They can also summarize their new learning, write lyrics or music, or research information about a musician or musical instrument.

Sharing

Don't forget to give your students opportunities to share with a partner, in small groups, or with the entire class after they have written in response to content curriculum. Time constraints can discourage us from doing this, but sharing is beneficial in so many ways.

It informs us of what the students learned.

It informs us of confusions or misunderstandings so that we can reteach the concepts.

It informs us of what students felt were important or interesting aspects.

It reinforces learning as students share with each other.

It gives students an opportunity to articulate and solidify their thoughts, opinions, and new learning.

And may I remind you just once more? We need to model, model, model! Write alongside your students. Demonstrate your thinking and responses. Never ask them to do something that you aren't willing to do yourself.

Don't limit yourself to the suggestions in this chapter. Rise to the challenge presented in Randy Bomer's quote at the beginning of this chapter. Make a list of ways to use the notebook with your students and try to outgrow that list. The more you use your notebooks, the more ideas you will generate.

Exchange ideas with your colleagues for expanding the use of your notebooks. Ask them what kinds of written responses work well for them and share what has worked well for you. Teachers are experts at borrowing ideas. One of my favorite quotes comes from an unknown author:

If you have an apple and I have an apple and we exchange apples, then you and I still each have one apple. But if you have an idea and I have an idea and we exchange ideas, then each of us still has two ideas.

Wise words for students and teachers to live by!

13 Refining the Use of the Writer's Notebook

I shall never assign journal writing to a class again.
Jean Little (1991, p. 126)

Jean Little recalls the harsh words spoken by a frustrated teacher. Haven't we all declared "Never again!" when we've failed to get the desired results? Jean's sixth-grade teacher was discouraged and upset with the boring entries that filled her students' journals. By anticipating some of the challenges that you may face as you use notebooks to support young writers, it is my hope that you will never feel like echoing the words of Little's disgruntled teacher.

Privacy Issues

Student privacy is one of the first things that teachers ask about, and rightfully so. We live in an age in which privacy is extensively protected. James Cross Giblin shares some advice:

> You can't write a journal if you're thinking of an audience first rather than yourself. A journal at its best should be a completely free and open conversation with yourself. You really have to trust yourself and open up if you're going to keep a journal. If you don't there's not much point in it. Ideally one should probably keep two journals—one for public consumption and another strictly private, where nothing needs to be left out.
>
> (cited in Graham, 1999, p. 49)

In a notebook entry, Jennifer, a seventh grader, expressed her desire to learn to speak English. She wanted to be able to communicate with people, but she found the English language difficult to learn. She revealed that she preferred to write rather than talk because she was afraid she would "talk wrong."

I followed Giblin's advice when one of my students revealed in an entry that she felt her grades were slipping because of something that had happened the previous year. I stumbled on this entry when I was showing the notebook to her mother at parent-teacher conferences. I expressed my surprise, because her grades were good and I had no idea that she was carrying a burden. Her mother explained what her daughter had experienced the previous year; she expressed concern that her daughter was still having difficulty dealing with it, even though she had received help.

This news left me saddened and angry. How could I allow my student to deal with this issue by writing about it but still respect her privacy? The next day, I decided to give her a special notebook that I had tucked away in my cupboard. I wrote her a note and explained how writing helps me cope with challenging things in my life. I also explained that this journal would be for her to keep at home—a place to write private thoughts for no one else to read. The words of poet Sara Holbrook helped emphasize my point:

> I use my journal for self-talk, a way to gain perspective when I'm frustrated. Writing it down helps me sort things out. It helps me keep my feet on the ground and my head going in the right way. It's also a place I go to dump toxic waste, which is why it would be so unfair for somebody to come along and read it. . . .
>
> The frustrations and anger I don't want to drag out in public I leave in my journal.
>
> Sarah Holbrook (cited in Graham, 1999, p. 151)

The following day, this student handed me a handwritten note that said, "Thank you very much for my notebook. It is very beautiful. My mom said it was neat when you said it helps you to write down things that bother you. I think that really helps me good. I wrote down what happened to me and how I feel. I took two pages to write about that."

Another way that students can request privacy is by folding their page in half (toward the spine). We need to honor these requests for privacy as we strive to maintain the trust and respect that we've built in our community of writers.

Writer's Block

Every writer has days when the well runs dry—there seems to be nothing to write about. It's helpful to brainstorm with your students about ways to get ideas flowing again when the drought hits. Students can list the ideas in the backs of their notebooks for future reference. Here are some possibilities that students have helped generate:

- Sketch.
- Make a list or web.
- Look at the "Ideas" page in your notebook.
- Reread entries in your notebook.

- Rewrite an entry and change the point of view.
- Look at books.
- Read classmates' stories or writing.
- Read or write poetry.
- Observe something or someone.
- Write down lyrics from a song that you know or make up your own lyrics.
- Use an artifact.
- Interview someone.
- Copy a quote and jot down the thoughts that it generates.
- Copy a line from an entry or a poem and write from it.
- Glue in a word, phrase, or picture from a magazine or newspaper and write about it.
- Look at a dictionary and add to your list of amazing words.
- Cut out an article or cartoon from the newspaper and write from it.
- Write down questions or wonderings.
- Look at an encyclopedia.
- Just begin writing—anything!

David Adler says, "Whenever I get stuck I just look at the sign I have over my desk: DON'T THINK! JUST WRITE!" (1999, p. 21). Lauren tried this last idea when she was struggling to think of something to write about at home one evening. Figure 13.1 shows the poem that evolved. Serena, a third grader, has learned what works for her when she feels stymied. She begins to write rows of "COCOCOCOC" until something happens—an idea comes to mind, and she begins to write.

Naomi Shihab Nye gives good advice for young writers when they are struggling: "I encourage them to start with a question. What three things would I like to remember about today? What do I care about that I haven't shared with anyone today? What worries me right now?" (cited in Graham, 1991, p. 205). Generate a list of questions with your students that will help them when they feel as though the well is dry.

English Language Learners

Our school district has a high percentage of students who are English language learners (ELLs). These students write in their notebooks in their first language and then transition gradually to English as they learn to express themselves. I encourage them to sketch as well as write. Not

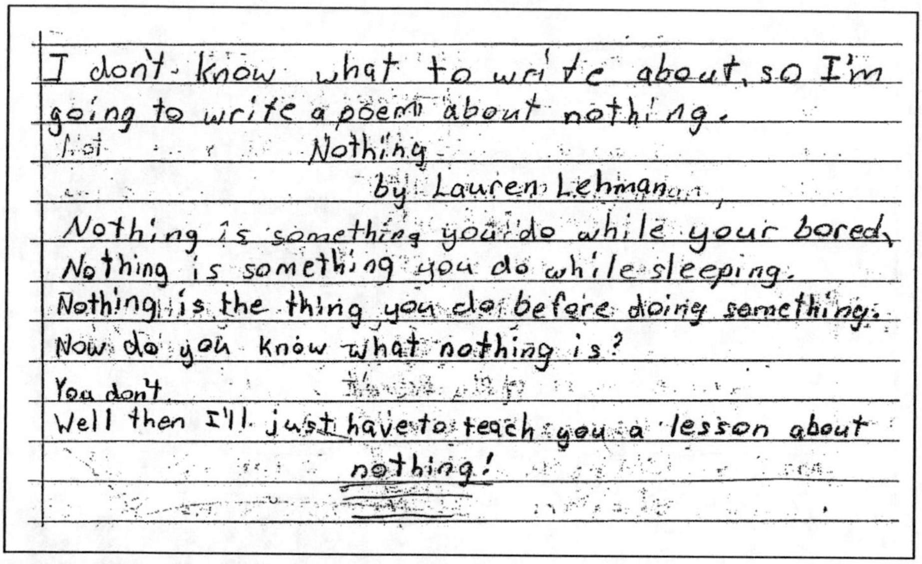

> I don't know what to write about, so I'm
> going to write a poem about nothing.
> list   Nothing
>   by Lauren Lehman
> Nothing is something you do while your bored,
> Nothing is something you do while sleeping.
> Nothing is the thing you do before doing something.
> Now do you know what nothing is?
> You don't
> Well then I'll just have to teach you a lesson about
>   nothing!

Figure 13.1. Lauren's poem.

only does this give them another way to express themselves, but it also helps me get the gist of what they are saying. Our bilingual teachers are also helpful in translating when necessary. It's important to give ELL students a voice and an opportunity to learn to use the notebook as a support for their writing. Figure 13.2 shows how one of my students felt when he left Mexico to come to the United States. His picture says it all.

Homework

My goal is to get students in the habit of writing in their writer's notebooks not only in school but also outside of school. Assigning notebook writing for homework helps students get in the habit of using the notebook in other settings and begin to live a writerly life. I try to balance the amount of writing between home and school—several entries in school and a couple for homework each week—so that they are usually making entries on a daily basis.

It's important to communicate with parents about your expectations regarding the notebook. A great way to do this is to have your students write a letter to their parents in their notebooks for open house or parent night. In their letters, they explain the purpose of the notebook and the expectations for writing in it. They can invite their parents to write a response in the notebook.

Figure 13.2. Edgar leaving Mexico.

Sometimes I give the class a topic or an idea to write about at home in case they can't generate an idea on their own. They know that they are always free to choose their own topic unless I give a specific assignment. This happens infrequently, and my students know they can always write more than one entry if they have something they want to write about.

What do you do if students don't do their homework? I deal with this the same way that I deal with other incomplete assignments. They write at recess or another appropriate time so that they know that they will be held accountable. I check to see if they have written an entry the morning after a notebook writing has been assigned. I check off their names on a chart if they have done it; this is part of my assessment, which I discuss in the next section.

Using Technology

Some writers use their computers for journaling. Sara Holbrook shares what works for her: "Writing on a computer is much faster for me. I have a few friends and authors I E-mail about my daily activities, joys, and frustrations—my daughter getting married, my dog getting hit by a car. I dump copies of my letters into Word Perfect files. Once a month I print them out and put them in a file" (cited in Graham, 1999, p. 151).

Children's poet, Rebecca Kai Dotlich, journals on her website once a month for her readers. (You can read her entries at http://www.rebeccakaidotlich.com.) Her entries are interesting and relevant to my life, and they give me ideas for my own writing.

Blogging has become a popular way to go public with personal journaling. It allows writers to put their thoughts online for others to read. It differs from the notebook because all of the entries are available for readers. Meg Cabot, award-winning writer of the Princess Diary series, encourages teenagers at her workshops to return to old-fashioned journals to vent so that no one gets hurt and too much information isn't given out. However, blogging may be the catalyst that some students need to begin writing (with discretion). Their entries can be printed and slipped into a binder or file.

Assessment

I never grade notebook writing because this writing is risk-free. However, I do assess for accountability and productivity. Whatever you use for assessment, keep it simple and useful for yourself and your students. Rubrics or checklists are two assessments that help me and also give students something to strive for.

A point system could look something like this:

10 points for writing outside of school (homework or writing on their own)

10 points for quality of entries (Are there honest attempts to write meaningful entries of appropriate length?)

10 points for a variety of entries

10 points for attitude toward using the notebook

10 points for being responsible for returning notebook to school and taking proper care of it

Total Points = 50

I assess the notebooks every nine weeks so that I can average in the points with other grades. I want students to know that I value what they are doing in a way that promotes, not hinders, our goals for them as writers.

More important than my assessment are the student reflections and self-assessments. They respond to such questions as the following:

> What kinds of entries (your choice) have you written in your notebook?
>
> What are your favorite topics to write about?
>
> What kinds of entries could you write in order to broaden your writing?
>
> Have you met the expectations for writing in your notebook outside of school?
>
> Have you been responsible for taking care of your notebook?
>
> What is your favorite kind of writing that you do in your notebook?

At the end of the year, I ask students to jot down their feelings about their notebooks.

> How did the notebook help you as a writer?
>
> How will you continue to use your notebook in the future?
>
> What does your notebook mean to you?

A way to celebrate is to give them time to read over their notebooks and chose one or two entries to share with a peer. Bring the exercise to closure by talking about how their notebooks hold moments of their lives and how these moments may be lost if they don't make a special effort to put their notebook in a place of safekeeping.

It takes time and patience to work through some of the challenges that arise as you begin using the writer's notebooks in your classrooms. Don't get discouraged if entries aren't always the quality you want, if a few notebooks get lost, or if some students are apathetic. You only have your writers in your class for one year; however, you never know which students will latch on to using notebooks for the rest of their lives.

The other day, this email was sent to me from a friend and colleague. Lisa wrote, "Just thought you might find this story heartwarming with your interest in writer's notebooks. It's a note I sent to Matt and Leslie about my daughter Leah who is 12." (Matt was Leah's teacher in fifth grade, and Leslie in sixth.)

> Hi Matt and Leslie,
>   Not long ago I took Leah to a Natalie Grant concert. There, in the dark, she rooted frantically through my purse and got out my

notebook. Using my cell phone as her light, she began to write with urgency. "What are you doing?" I asked.

"I just had to write down some of those words for my collection," she answered. I was thrilled at the sight, because I witnessed an authentic urge within her and an ability to recognize something she deemed worth keeping. Throughout the concert, she filled three pages with words, phrases, and lyrics she didn't want to forget. Later, I saw her transferring them into her writer's notebook. No doubt they will show up some day in her own writing. As a writing teacher myself, my goal has long been to nurture a desire within my own kids. That night I saw a glimpse of it. Thank you so much for the very large part you have both played in fanning that writing flame.

Warmly,
Lisa

You could be the teacher that changes a child forever, simply by introducing the notebook as an avenue to express a voice, make sense of one's life, and become a lifelong writer. Will you be the one to fan the flame?

Appendix

NCTE Beliefs about the Teaching of Writing

by the Writing Study Group of the NCTE Executive Committee
November 2004

Just as the nature of and expectation for literacy has changed in the past century and a half, so has the nature of writing. Much of that change has been due to technological developments, from pen and paper, to typewriter, to word processor, to networked computer, to design software capable of composing words, images, and sounds. These developments not only expanded the types of texts that writers produce, they also expanded immediate access to a wider variety of readers. With full recognition that writing is an increasingly multifaceted activity, we offer several principles that should guide effective teaching practice.

1. Everyone has the capacity to write, writing can be taught, and teachers can help students become better writers.

Though poets and novelists may enjoy debating whether or not writing can be taught, teachers of writing have more pragmatic aims. Setting aside the question of whether one can learn to be an artistic genius, there is ample empirical evidence that anyone can get better at writing, and that what teachers do makes a difference in how much students are capable of achieving as writers.

Developing writers require support. This support can best come through carefully designed writing instruction oriented toward acquiring new strategies and skills. Certainly, writers can benefit from teachers who simply support and give them time to write. However, instruction matters. Teachers of writing should be well-versed in composition theory and research, and they should know methods for turning that theory into practice. When writing teachers first walk into classrooms, they should already know and practice good composition. However, much as in doctoring, learning to teach well is a lifetime process, and lifetime professional development is the key to successful practice. Students deserve no less.

2. People learn to write by writing.

As is the case with many other things people do, getting better at writing requires doing it—a lot. This means actual writing, not merely listening to lectures about writing, doing grammar drills, or discussing readings. The more people write, the easier it gets and the more they are motivated to do it. Writers who write a lot learn more about the process because they have had more experience inside it. Writers learn from each session with their hands on a keyboard or around a pencil as they draft, rethink, revise, and draft again. Thinking about how to make your writing better is what revision is. In other words, improvement is built into the experience of writing.

What does this mean for teaching?

Writing instruction must include ample in-class and out-of-class opportunities for writing and should include writing for a variety of purposes and audiences.

Writing, though, should not be viewed as an activity that happens only within a classroom's walls. Teachers need to support students in the development of writing lives, habits, and preferences for life outside school. We already know that many students do extensive amounts of self-sponsored writing: emailing, keeping journals or doing creative projects, instant messaging, making Web sites, blogging and so on. As much as possible, instruction should be geared toward making sense in a life outside of school, so that writing has ample room to grow in individuals' lives. It is useful for teachers to consider what elements of their curriculum they could imagine students self-sponsoring outside of school. Ultimately, those are the activities that will produce more writing.

In order to provide quality opportunities for student writing, teachers must minimally understand:

- How to interpret curriculum documents, including things that can be taught while students are actually writing, rather than one thing at a time to all students at once.
- The elements of "writing lives" as people construct them in the world outside of school.
- Social structures that support independent work.
- How to confer with individual writers.
- How to assess while students are writing.
- How to plan what students need to know in response to ongoing research.
- How to create a sense of personal safety in the classroom, so that students are willing to write freely and at length.
- How to create community while students are writing in the same room together.

3. Writing is a process.

Often, when people think of writing, they think of texts—finished pieces of writing. Understanding what writers do, however, involves thinking not just about what texts look like when they are finished but also about what strategies writers might employ to produce those texts. Knowledge about writing is only complete with understanding the complex of actions in which writers engage as they produce texts. Such understanding has two aspects. First is the development, through extended practice over years, of a repertory of routines, skills, strategies, and practices, for generating, revising, and editing different kinds of texts. Second is the development of reflective abilities and meta-awareness about writing. This procedural understanding helps writers most when they encounter difficulty, or when they are in the middle of creating a piece of writing. How does someone get started? What do they do when they get stuck? How do they plan the overall process, each section of their work, and even the rest of the sentence they are writing right now? Research, theory, and practice over the past 40 years has produced a richer understanding of what writers do—those who are proficient and professional as well as those who struggle.

Two further points are vital. To say that writing is a process is decidedly not to say that it should—or can—be turned into a formulaic set of steps. Experienced writers shift between different operations according to tasks and circumstances. Second, writers do not accumulate process skills and strategies once and for all. They develop and refine writing skills throughout their writing lives.

What does this mean for teaching?

Whenever possible, teachers should attend to the process that students might follow to produce texts—and not only specify criteria for evaluating finished products, in form or content. Students should become comfortable with prewriting techniques, multiple strategies for developing and organizing a message, a variety of strategies for revising and editing, and strategies for preparing products for public audiences and for deadlines. In explaining assignments, teachers should provide guidance and options for ways of going about it. Sometimes, evaluating the processes students follow—the decisions they make, the attempts along the way—can be as important as evaluating the final product. At least some of the time, the teacher should guide the students through the process, assisting them as they go. Writing instruction must provide opportunities for students to identify the processes that work best for themselves as they move from one writing situation to another.

Writing instruction must also take into account that a good deal of workplace writing and other writing takes place in collaborative situations. Writers must learn to work effectively with one another.

Teachers need to understand at least the following in order to be excellent at teaching writing as a process:

- The relationship between features of finished writing and the actions writers perform.
- What writers of different genres say about their craft.

- The process of writing from the inside, that is, what they themselves as writers experience in a host of different writing situations.
- Multiple strategies for approaching a wide range of typical problems writers face during composing, including strategies for audience and task analysis, invention, revision, and editing.
- Multiple models of the writing process, the varied ways individuals approach similar tasks, and the ways that writing situations and genres inform processes.
- Published texts, immediately available, that demonstrate a wide range of writing strategies and elements of craft.
- The relationships among the writing process, curriculum, learning, and pedagogy.
- How to design time for students to do their best work on an assignment.
- How writers use tools, including word-processing and design software and computer-based resources.

4. Writing is a tool for thinking.

When writers actually write, they think of things that they did not have in mind before they began writing. The act of writing generates ideas. This is different from the way we often think of writers—as getting ideas fixed in their heads before they write them down. The notion that writing is a medium for thought is important in several ways. It suggests a number of important uses for writing: to solve problems, to identify issues, to construct questions, to reconsider something one had already figured out, to try out a half-baked idea. This insight that writing is a tool for thinking helps us to understand the process of drafting and revision as one of exploration and discovery, and is nothing like transcribing from pre-recorded tape. The writing process is not one of simply fixing up the mistakes in an early draft, but of finding more and more wrinkles and implications in what one is talking about.

What does this mean for teaching?

In any writing classroom, some of the writing is for others and some of the writing is for the writer. Regardless of the age, ability, or experience of the writer, the use of writing to generate thought is still valuable; therefore, forms of writing such as personal narrative, journals, written reflections, observations, and writing-to-learn strategies are important.

In any writing assignment, it must be assumed that part of the work of writers will involve generating and regenerating ideas prior to writing them.

Excellence in teaching writing as thinking requires that the teacher understand:

- Varied tools for thinking through writing, such as journals, writers' notebooks, blogs, sketchbooks, digital portfolios, listservs or online discussion groups, dialogue journals, double-entry or dialectical journals, and others.

- The kinds of new thinking that occur when writers revise.

- The variety of types of thinking people do when they compose, and what those types of thinking look like when they appear in writing.

- Strategies for getting started with an idea, or finding an idea when one does not occur immediately.

5. Writing grows out of many different purposes.

Purposes for writing include developing social networks; engaging in civic discourse; supporting personal and spiritual growth; reflecting on experience; communicating professionally and academically; building relationships with others, including friends, family, and like-minded individuals; and engaging in aesthetic experiences.

Writing is not just one thing. It varies in form, structure, and production process according to its audience and purpose. A note to a cousin is not like a business report, which is different again from a poem. The processes and ways of thinking that lead up to these varied kinds of texts can also vary widely, from the quick single draft email to a friend to the careful drafting and redrafting of a legal contract. The different purposes and forms both grow out of and create various relationships between the writer and the potential reader, and relationships reflected in degrees of formality in language, as well as assumptions about what knowledge and experience is already shared, and what needs to be explained. Writing with certain purposes in mind, the writer focuses her attention on what the audience is thinking or believing; other times, the writer focuses more on the information she is organizing, or on her own thoughts and feelings. Therefore, the thinking, the procedures, and the physical format in writing all differ when writers' purposes vary.

What does this mean for teaching?

Often, in school, students write only to prove that they did something they were asked to do, in order to get credit for it. Or, students are taught a single type of writing and are led to believe this type will suffice in all situations. Writers outside of school have many different purposes beyond demonstrating accountability, and they practice myriad types and genres. In order to make sure students are learning how writing differs when the purpose and the audience differ, it is important that teachers create opportunities for students to be in different kinds of writing situations, where the relationships and agendas are varied. Even within academic settings, the characteristics of good writing vary among disciplines; what counts as a successful lab report, for example, differs from a successful history paper, essay exam, or literary interpretation.

In order to teach for excellence about purposes in writing, teachers need to understand:

- The wide range of purposes for which people write, and the forms of writing that arise from those purposes.

- Strategies and forms for writing for public participation in a democratic society.

- Ways people use writing for personal growth, expression, and reflection and how to encourage and develop this kind of writing.

- Aesthetic or artistic forms of writing and how they are made. That is, the production of creative and literary texts, for the purposes of entertainment, pleasure, or exploration.

- Appropriate forms for varied academic disciplines and the purposes and relationships that create those forms.

- Ways of organizing and transforming school curricula in order to provide students with adequate education in varied purposes for writing.

- How to set up a course to write for varied purposes and audiences.

6. Conventions of finished and edited texts are important to readers and therefore to writers.

Readers expect writing to conform to their expectations, to match the conventions generally established for public texts. Contemporary readers expect words to be spelled in a standardized way, for punctuation to be used in predictable ways, for usage and syntax to match that used in texts they already acknowledge as successful. They expect the style in a piece of writing to be appropriate to its genre and social situation. In other words, it is important that writing that goes public be "correct."

What does this mean for teaching?

Every teacher has to resolve a tension between writing as generating and shaping ideas and writing as demonstrating expected surface conventions. On the one hand, it is important for writing to be as correct as possible and for students to be able to produce correct texts. On the other hand, achieving correctness is only one set of things writers must be able to do; a correct text empty of ideas or unsuited to its audience or purpose is not a good piece of writing. There is no formula for resolving this tension. Writing is both/and: both fluency and fitting conventions. Research shows that facility in these two operations often develops unevenly. For example, as students learn increasingly sophisticated ways of thinking (for example, conditional or subordinate reasoning) or dealing with unfamiliar content, they may produce more surface errors, or perhaps even seem to regress. This is because their mental energies are focused on the new intellectual challenges. Such uneven development is to be tolerated, in fact, encouraged. It is rather like strength gains from lifting weight, which actually tears down muscle fibers only to stimulate them to grow back stronger. Too much emphasis on correctness can actually inhibit development. By the same token, without mastering conventions for written discourse, writers' efforts may come to naught. Drawing readers' attention to the gap between the text at hand and the qualities of texts they expect causes readers to not attend to the content. Each teacher must be knowledgeable enough about the entire landscape of writing instruction to guide particular students toward a goal, developing both increasing fluency in new contexts and mastery of conventions. NCTE's stated policy over many years has been that conventions of writing are best taught in the context of writing. Simply completing workbook or online exercises is inadequate if students are not regularly producing meaningful texts themselves.

Most writing teachers teach students how to edit their writing that will go out to audiences. This is often considered a late stage in the process of composing, because editing is only essential for the words that are left after all the cutting, replacing, rewriting, and adding that go on during revision. Writers need an image in their minds of conventional grammar, spelling, and punctuation in order to compare what is already on the page to an ideal of correctness. They also need to be aware of stylistic options that will produce the most desirable impression on their readers. All of the dimensions of editing are motivated by a concern for an audience. Teachers should be familiar with techniques for teaching editing and encouraging reflective knowledge about editing conventions. For example, some find it useful to have students review a collection of their writing over time—a journal, notebook, folder, or portfolio—to study empirically the way their writing has changed or needs to change, with respect to conventions. A teacher might say, "let's look at all the times you used commas," or "investigate the ways you might have combined sentences." Such reflective appointments permit students to set goals for their own improvement.

Teachers need to understand at least the following in order to be excellent at teaching conventions to writers:

- Research on developmental factors in writing ability, including the tension between fluency with new operations or contents and the practice of accepted spelling, punctuation, syntactic, and usage conventions.
- The diverse influences and constraints on writers' decision making as they determine the kinds of conventions that apply to this situation and this piece of writing.
- A variety of applications and options for most conventions.
- The appropriate conventions for academic classroom English.
- How to teach usage without excessive linguistic terminology.
- The linguistic terminology that is necessary for teaching particular kinds of usage.

- The linguistic terminology necessary for communicating pro-fessionally with other educators.

- The relationship among rhetorical considerations and decisions about conventions, for example, the conditions under which a dash, a comma, a semi-colon, or a full stop might be more effec-tive.

- Conventions beyond the sentence, such as effective uses of bulleted lists, mixed genres and voices, diagrams and charts, design of pages, and composition of video shots.

- An understanding of the relationship among conventions in primary and secondary discourses.

- The conditions under which people learn to do new things with language.

- The relationship among fluency, clarity, and correctness in writ-ing development and the ability to assess which is the leading edge of the student's learning now.

7. Writing and reading are related.

Writing and reading are related. People who read a lot have a much easier time getting better at writing. In order to write a particular kind of text, it helps if the writer has read that kind of text. In order to take on a particular style of language, the writer needs to have read that language, to have heard it in her mind, so that she can hear it again in order to compose it.

Writing can also help people become better readers. In their earliest writing experiences, children listen for the relationships of sounds to letters, which contributes greatly to their phonemic awareness and phonics knowledge. Writers also must learn how texts are structured, because they have to create them. The experience of plotting a short story, organizing a research report, or making line breaks in a poem permits the writer, as a reader, to approach new reading experiences with more informed eyes.

Additionally, reading is a vital source of information and ideas. For writers fully to contribute to a given topic or to be effective in a given situation, they must be familiar with what previous writers have said. Reading also creates a sense of what one's audience knows or expects on a topic.

What does this mean for teaching?

One way to help students become better writers is to make sure they have lots of extended time to read, in school and out. Most research indicates that the easiest way to tap motivation to read is to teach students to choose books and other texts they understand and enjoy, and then to give them time in school to read them. In addition to making students stronger readers, this practice makes them stronger writers.

Students should also have access to and experience in reading material that presents both published and student writing in various genres. Through immersion in a genre, students develop an internalized sense of why an author would select a particular genre for a particular purpose, the power of a particular genre to convey a message, and the rhetorical constraints and possibilities inherent in a genre. Students should be taught the features of different genres, experientially not only explicitly, so that they develop facilities in producing them and become familiar with variant features. If one is going to write in a genre, it is very helpful to have read in that genre first.

Overall, frequent conversations about the connections between what we read and what we write are helpful. These connections will sometimes be about the structure and craft of the writing itself, and sometimes about thematic and content connections.

In order to do an excellent job of teaching into the connections of writing and reading, teachers need to understand at least these things:

- How writers read in a special way, with an eye toward not just what the text says but how it is put together.
- The psychological and social processes reading and writing have in common.
- The ways writers form and use constructs of their intended readers, anticipating their responses and needs.
- An understanding of text structure that is fluid enough to accommodate frequent disruptions.

8. Writing has a complex relationship to talk.

From its beginnings in early childhood through the most complex setting imaginable, writing exists in a nest of talk. Conversely, speakers usually write notes and, regularly, scripts, and they often prepare visual materials that include texts and images. Writers often talk in order to rehearse the language and content that will go into what they write, and conversation often provides an impetus or occasion for writing. They sometimes confer with teachers and other writers about what to do next, how to improve their drafts, or in order to clarify their ideas and purposes. Their usual ways of speaking sometimes do and sometimes do not feed into the sentences they write, depending on an intricate set of decisions writers make continually. One of the features of writing that is most evident and yet most difficult to discuss is the degree to which it has "voice." The fact that we use this term, even in the absence of actual sound waves, reveals some of the special relationship between speech and writing.

What does this mean for teaching?

In early writing, we can expect lots of talk to surround writing, since what children are doing is figuring out how to get speech onto paper. Early teaching in composition should also attend to helping children get used to producing language orally, through telling stories, explaining how things work, predicting what will happen, and guessing about why things and people are the way they are. Early writing experiences will include students explaining orally what is in a text, whether it is printed or drawn.

As they grow, writers still need opportunities to talk about what they are writing about, to rehearse the language of their upcoming texts and run ideas by trusted colleagues before taking the risk of committing words to paper. After making a draft, it is often helpful for writers to discuss with peers what they have done, partly in order to get ideas from their peers, partly to see what they, the writers, say when they try to explain their thinking. Writing conferences, wherein student writers talk about their work with a teacher, who can make suggestions or re-orient what the writer is doing, are also very helpful uses of talk in the writing process.

To take advantage of the strong relationships between talk and writing, teachers must minimally understand:

- Ways of setting up and managing student talk in partnerships and groups.
- Ways of establishing a balance between talk and writing in classroom management.
- Ways of organizing the classroom and/or schedule to permit individual teacher-student conferences.
- Strategies for deliberate insertions of opportunities for talk into the writing process: knowing when and how students should talk about their writing.
- Ways of anticipating and solving interpersonal conflicts that arise when students discuss writing.
- Group dynamics in classrooms.
- Relationships—both similarities and differences—between oral and literate language.
- The uses of writing in public presentations and the values of students making oral presentations that grow out of and use their writing.

9. Literate practices are embedded in complicated social relationships.

Writing happens in the midst of a web of relationships. There is, most obviously, the relationship between the writer and the reader. That relationship is often very specific: writers have a definite idea of who will read their words, not just a generalized notion that their text will be available to the world. Furthermore, particular people surround the writer—other writers, partners in purposes, friends, members of a given community—during the process of composing. They may know what the writer is doing and be indirectly involved in it, though they are not the audience for the work. In workplace and academic settings, writers write because someone in authority tells them to. Therefore, power relationships are built into the writing situation. In every writing situation, the writer, the reader, and all relevant others live in a structured social order, where some people's words count more than others, where being heard is more difficult for some people than others, where some people's words come true and others' do not.

Writers start in different places. It makes a difference what kind of language a writer spoke while growing up, and what kinds of language they are being asked to take on later in their experience. It makes a difference, too, the culture a writer comes from, the ways people use language in that culture and the degree to which that culture is privileged in the larger society. Important cultural differences are not only ethnic but also racial, economic, geographical and ideological. For example, rural students from small communities will have different language experiences than suburban students from comprehensive high schools, and students who come from very conservative backgrounds where certain texts are privileged or excluded will have different language experiences than those from progressive backgrounds where the same is true. How much a writer has access to wide, diverse experiences and means of communication creates predispositions and skill for composing for an audience.

What does this mean for teaching?

The teaching of writing should assume students will begin with the sort of language with which they are most at home and most fluent in their speech. That language may be a dialect of English, or even a different language altogether. The goal is not to leave students where they are, however, but to move them toward greater flexibility, so that they can write not just for their own intimates but for wider audiences. Even as they move toward more widely-used English, it is not necessary or desirable to wipe out the ways their family and neighborhood of origin use words. The teaching of excellence in writing means adding language to what already exists, not subtracting. The goal is to make more relationships available, not fewer.

In order to teach for excellence, a writing teacher needs understandings like these about contexts of language:

- How to find out about a students' language use in the home and neighborhoods, the changes in language context they may have encountered in their lives, and the kinds of language they most value.

- That wider social situations in which students write, speak, read, and relate to other people affect what seems "natural" or "easy" to them — or not.

- How to discuss with students the need for flexibility in the employment of different kinds of language for different social contexts.

- How to help students negotiate maintenance of their most familiar language while mastering academic classroom English and the varieties of English used globally.

- Control and awareness of their own varied languages and linguistic contexts.
- An understanding of the relationships among group affiliation, identity, and language.
- Knowledge of the usual patterns of common dialects in English, such as African American English, Spanish and varieties of English related to Spanish, common patterns in American rural and urban populations, predictable patterns in the English varieties of groups common in their teaching contexts.
- How and why to study a community's ways of using language.

10. Composing occurs in different modalities and technologies.

Increasingly rapid changes in technologies mean that composing is involving a combination of modalities, such as print, still images, video, and sound. Computers make it possible for these modalities to combine in the same work environment. Connections to the Internet not only make a range of materials available to writers, they also collapse distances between writers and readers and between generating words and creating designs. Print always has a visual component, even if it is only the arrangement of text on a page and the type font. Furthermore, throughout history, print has often been partnered with pictures in order to convey more meaning, to add attractiveness, and to appeal to a wider audience. Television, video, and film all involve such combinations, as do websites and presentation software. As basic tools for communicating expand to include modes beyond print alone, "writing" comes to mean more than scratching words with pen and paper. Writers need to be able to think about the physical design of text, about the appropriateness and thematic content of visual images, about the integration of sound with a reading experience, and about the medium that is most appropriate for a particular message, purpose, and audience.

What does this mean for teaching?

Writing instruction must accommodate the explosion in technology from the world around us.

From the use of basic word processing to support drafting, revision, and editing to the use of hypertext and the infusion of visual components in writing, the definition of what writing instruction includes must evolve to embrace new requirements.

Many teachers and students do not, however, have adequate access to computing, recording, and video equipment to take advantage of the most up-to-date technologies. In many cases, teaching about the multi-modal nature of writing is best accomplished through varying the forms of writing with more ordinary implements. Writing picture books allows students to think between text and images, considering the ways they work together and distribute the reader's attention. Similar kinds of visual/verbal thinking can be supported through other illustrated text forms, including some kinds of journals/sketchbooks and posters. In addition, writing for performance requires the writer to imagine what the audience will see and hear and thus draws upon multiple modes of thinking, even in the production of a print text. Such uses of technology without the latest equipment reveal the extent to which "new" literacies are rooted also in older ones.

Teachers need to understand at least the following in order to be excellent at teaching composition as involving multiple media:

- A range of new genres that have emerged with the increase in electronic communication. Because these genres are continually evolving, this knowledge must be continually updated.

- Operation of some of the hardware and software their students will use, including resources for solving software and hardware problems.

- Internet resources for remaining up to date on technologies.

- Design principles for Web pages.

- E-mail and chat conventions.

- How to navigate both the World Wide Web and web-based databases.

- The use of software for making Web sites, including basic html, such as how to make a link.

- Theory about the relationship between print and other modalities.

11. Assessment of writing involves complex, informed, human judgment.

Assessment of writing occurs for different purposes. Sometimes, a teacher assesses in order to decide what the student has achieved and what he or she still needs to learn. Sometimes, an entity beyond the classroom assesses a student's level of achievement in order to say whether they can go on to some new educational level that requires the writer to be able to do certain things. At other times, school authorities require a writing test in order to pressure teachers to teach writing. Still other times, as in a history exam, the assessment of writing itself is not the point, but the quality of the writing is evaluated almost in passing. In any of these assessments of writing, complex judgments are formed. Such judgments should be made by human beings, not machines. Furthermore, they should be made by professionals who are informed about writing, development, and the field of literacy education.

What does this mean for teaching?

Instructors of composition should know about various methods of assessment of student writing. Instructors must recognize the difference between formative and summative evaluation and be prepared to evaluate students' writing from both perspectives. By formative evaluation here, we mean provisional, ongoing, in-process judgments about what students know and what to teach next. By summative evaluation, we mean final judgments about the quality of student work. Teachers of writing must also be able to recognize the developmental aspects of writing ability and devise appropriate lessons for students at all levels of expertise.

Teachers need to understand at least the following in order to be excellent at writing assessment:

- How to find out what student writers can do, informally, on an ongoing basis.
- How to use that assessment in order to decide what and how to teach next.
- How to assess occasionally, less frequently than above, in order to form judgments about the quality of student writing and learning.
- How to assess ability and knowledge across multiple different writing engagements.
- What the features of good writing are, appropriate to the context and purposes of the teaching and learning.
- What the elements of a constructive process of writing are, appropriate to the context and purposes of the teaching and learning.
- What growth in writing looks like, the developmental aspects of writing ability.
- Ways of assessing student metacognitive process of the reading/writing connection.
- How to recognize in student writing (both in their texts and in their actions) the nascent potential for excellence at the features and processes desired.
- How to deliver useful feedback, appropriate for the writer and the situation.
- How to analyze writing situations for their most essential elements, so that assessment is not of everything about writing all at once, but rather is targeted to objectives.
- How to analyze and interpret both qualitative and quantitative writing assessments.
- How to evaluate electronic texts.
- How to use portfolios to assist writers in their development.
- How self-assessment and reflection contribute to a writer's development and ability to move among genres, media, and rhetorical situations.

Works Cited

Ada, A. F. (1995). *My name is Maria Isabel*. New York: Aladdin/Simon & Schuster.

Adler, D. A. (1999). *My writing day*. Katonah, NY: Owen.

Alphin, E. M. (2000). *Creating characters kids will love*. Cincinnati, OH: Writer's Digest Books/F&W Publications.

Anderson, C. (2000). *How's it going? A practical guide to conferring with student writers*. Portsmouth, NH: Heinemann.

Anderson, C. (2005). *Assessing writers*. Portsmouth, NH: Heinemann.

Angelillo, J. (2002). *A fresh approach to teaching punctuation*. New York: Scholastic.

Arnosky, J. (1988). *Sketching outdoors in winter*. New York: Lothrop, Lee & Shepard.

Avi. (2001). *The secret school*. New York: Harcourt.

Bentley, W. A. (2000). *Snowflakes in photographs*. New York: Dover.

Blume, J. (1985). *The pain and the great one*. New York: Simon & Schuster.

Bohlke, L. B., ed. (1986). *Willa Cather in person: Interviews, speeches, and letters*. Lincoln: U of Nebraska P.

Bomer, K. (2005). *Writing a life: Teaching memoir to sharpen insight, shape meaning—and triumph over tests*. Portsmouth, NH: Heinemann.

Bomer, R. (1995). *Time for meaning: Crafting literate lives in middle and high school*. Portsmouth, NH: Heinemann.

Bomer, R., & Bomer, K. (2001). *For a better world: Reading and writing for social action*. Portsmouth, NH: Heinemann.

Boynton, S. (1984). *Blue hat, green hat*. New York: Little Simon Books/Simon & Schuster.

Brammer, E. C. (2002). *My Tata's guitar*. Houston, TX: Piñata Books.

Brinckloe, J. (1986). *Fireflies!* New York: Aladdin/Simon & Schuster.

Brisson, P. (1998). *The summer my father was ten*. Honesdale, PA: Boyds Mills Press.

Bunting, E. (1994). *Sunshine home*. New York: Clarion Books/Houghton Mifflin.

Bunting, E. (1996). *The secret place*. New York: Clarion Books/Houghton Mifflin.

Bunting, E. (2000). *The memory string*. New York: Clarion Books/Houghton Mifflin.

Bunting, E. (2002). *One candle*. New York: Cotler Books/HarperCollins.

Calkins, L. M. (with Harwayne, S.). (1991). *Living between the lines*. Portsmouth, NH: Heinemann.

Calkins, L. M. Staff Development Resources (Booklet). Torrance, CA.

Choi, Y. (2003). *The name jar*. Cleveland, OH: Dell Dragonfly Books/Random House.

Cisneros, S. (1984). *The house on Mango Street*. New York: Random House.

Cleary, B. (1996). *A girl from Yamhill*. New York: Avon Books/HarperCollins.

Codell, E. R. (2003). *Sahara special*. New York: Hyperion Books.

Craig, S. (2002). *Sports writing: A beginner's guide*. Shoreham, VT: Discover Writing Press.

Cullinan, B. E. (Ed.). (1996). *A jar of tiny stars: Poems by NCTE award-winning poets*. Honesdale, PA: Boyds Mills Press.

cummings, e. e. (n.d.). [Quote]. Retrieved June 6, 2008, from http://www.brainyquote.com/quotes/authors/e/e_e_cummings.html

Dahl, R. (1999). *Boy: Tales of childhood*. New York: Puffin Books/Penguin.

de Regniers, B. S. (1988). *The way I feel sometimes*. New York: Clarion Books/Houghton Mifflin.

dePaola, T. (1993). *Tom*. New York: Putnam's Sons.

Ehrlich, A. (Ed.). (2002). *When I was your age: Original stories about growing up* (Vol. 2). Cambridge, MA: Candlewick Press.

Erasmus, Desiderius. (n.d.). [Quote]. Retrieved June 6, 2008, from http://www.brainyquote.com/quotes/quotes/d/desiderius124392.html

Fletcher, R. (1996). *A writer's notebook: Unlocking the writer within you*. New York: Avon Books/HarperCollins.

Fletcher, R. (2005). *Marshfield dreams: When I was a kid*. New York: Holt.

Fletcher, R. (2006a). *Boy writers: Reclaiming their voices*. Portland, ME: Stenhouse.

Fletcher, R. (2006b). *Reflections*. Katonah, NY: Owen.

Fletcher, R. (July, 2007). [keynote address]. "Creating Boy-Friendly Writing Classrooms." Keynote address presented at the 7th Annual Summer Literacy Institute of the Purdue Literacy Network Project, West Lafayette, IN.

Fletcher, R., & Portalupi, J. (1998). *Craft lessons: Teaching writing k–8*. Portland, ME: Stenhouse.

Fletcher, R., & Portalupi, J. (2001). *Writing workshop: The essential guide*. Portsmouth, NH: Heinemann.

Florian, D. (1999). *Winter eyes*. New York: Greenwillow Books/HarperCollins.

Florian, D. (2002). *Summersaults*. New York: Greenwillow Books/HarperCollins.

Florian, D. (2006). *Handsprings*. New York: Greenwillow Books/HarperCollins.

Fox, M. (1993). *Radical reflections: Passionate opinions on teaching, learning, and living.* Orlando, FL: Harvest Books/Harcourt.

Fraustino, L. R. (2001). *The hickory chair.* New York: Levine Books/Scholastic Press.

Garza, C. L. (2000). *In my family/En mi familia.* San Francisco: Children's Book Press.

Garza, C. L. (2005). *Family pictures.* San Francisco: Children's Book Press.

Gellman, M. (2000). *"Always wear clean underwear!" and other ways parents say "I love you."* New York: HarperTrophy/HarperCollins.

Graham, P. W. (1999). *Speaking of journals: Children's book writers talk about their diaries, notebooks, and sketchbooks.* Honesdale, PA: Boyds Mills Press.

Harper, I. (1995). *My cats Nick and Nora.* New York: Blue Sky Press/Scholastic.

Heard, G. (1999). *Awakening the heart: Exploring poetry in elementary and middle school.* Portsmouth, NH: Heinemann.

Hesse, K. (1999). *Come on, rain!* New York: Scholastic Press.

Holbrook, S. (2005). *Practical poetry: A nonstandard approach to meeting content-area standards.* Portsmouth, NH: Heinemann.

Indiana Department of Education. (2000). *Indiana's academic standards: Science.* Indianapolis, IN: Author.

Indiana Department of Education. (2001). *Indiana's academic standards: Social studies.* Indianapolis, IN: Author.

Indiana Department of Education. (2006). *Indiana's academic standards: English/language arts.* Indianapolis, IN: Author.

Janeczko, P. B. (1999). *How to write poetry.* New York: Scholastic.

Jiménez, F. (1997). *The circuit: Stories from the life of a migrant child.* Albuquerque: University of New Mexico Press.

Jiménez, F. (2000). *The Christmas gift.* Boston: Houghton Mifflin.

Johnston, P. H. (2004). *Choice words: How our language affects children's learning.* Portland, ME: Stenhouse.

Kehret, P. (2000). *Small steps: The year I got polio.* Morton Grove, IL: Whitman.

Kehret, P. (2001). *Cages.* New York: Puffin Books/Penguin.

Kehret, P. (2002). *Five pages a day: A writer's journey.* Morton Grove, IL: Whitman.

Kinney, J. (2007). *Diary of a wimpy kid.* New York: Amulet Books/Abrams.

Lamott, A. (1995). *Bird by bird: Some instructions on writing and life.* New York: Anchor Books/Random House.

Leslie, C. W. (2002). *Nature all year long.* Dubuque, IA. Kendall/Hunt.

Lichtenheld, T. (2003). *What are you so grumpy about?* New York: Little, Brown.

Little, J. (1990). *Hey world, here I am!* New York: HarperTrophy/HarperCollins.

Little, J. (1991). *Little by little: A writer's education*. New York: Puffin Books/ Penguin.

London, J., & London, A. (2001). *White water*. New York: Viking.

Lorbiecki, M. (2000). *Sister Anne's hands*. New York: Puffin Books/Penguin.

Lowry, L. (2000). *Looking back: A book of memories*. New York: Delacorte Press/ Random House.

Lowry, L. (2002). *Gooney bird green*. New York: Lorraine Books/Houghton Mifflin.

Lyon, G. E. (1999) *Where I'm from: Where poems come from*. Sprint, TX: Absey.

MacLachlan, P. (1994). *All the places to love*. New York: HarperCollins.

Martin, J. B. (1998). *Snowflake Bentley*. Boston: Houghton Mifflin.

Meyerowitz, J. (1985). *A summer's day*. New York: Times Books.

Moss, M. (1995). *Amelia's notebook*. Berkeley, CA: Tricycle Press/Ten Speed Press.

Moss, M. (2003). *Max's logbook*. New York: Scholastic Press.

Munson, D. (2000). *Enemy pie*. San Francisco: Chronicle Books.

Newkirk, T. (2002). *Misreading masculinity: Boys, literacy, and popular culture*. Portsmouth, NH: Heinemann.

Oliver, M. (1992). "The summer day." In *New and selected poems* (p. 94). Boston: Beacon.

O'Neill, M. (1989). *Hailstones and halibut bones*. New York: The Trumpet Club.

Pearson, P. D., & Gallagher, M. C. (1983). The instruction of reading comprehension. *Contemporary Educational Psychology, 8*, 317–344.

Pérez, A. I. (2008). *My very own room*. San Francisco: Children's Book Press.

Pittman, H. C. (1988). *Once when I was scared*. New York: Dutton.

Polacco, P. (1998). *Thank you, Mr. Falker*. New York: Scholastic.

Portalupi, J., & Fletcher, R. (2001). *Nonfiction craft lessons: Teaching information writing k–8*. Portland, ME: Stenhouse.

Portalupi, J., & Fletcher, R. (2004). *Teaching the qualities of writing: Ideas, design, language, presentation*. Portsmouth, NH: Heinemann.

Ray, K. W. (1999). *Wondrous words: Writers and writing in the elementary classroom*. Urbana, IL: National Council of Teachers of English.

Ray, K. W. (2006). *Study driven: A framework for planning units of study in the writing workshop*. Portsmouth, NH: Heinemann.

Recorvits, H. (2003). *My name is Yoon*. New York: Foster Books/Farrar, Straus and Giroux.

Rief, L. (1998). *Vision and voice: Extending the literary spectrum*. Portsmouth, NH: Heinemann.

Rubenstein, A. (2004, February 26). "Frank McCourt pays surprise visit to SBU." *The Statesman*. Retrieved June 6, 2008, from http://media.www.sbstatesman.com/media/storage/paper955/news/2004/02/26/CampusNews/Frank.Mccourt.Pays.Surprise.Visit.To.Sbu-1996301.shtml

Ruurs, M. (2001). *The Power of Poems: Teaching the joy of writing poetry*. Gainesville, FL: Maupin House.

Rylant, C. (1982). *When I was young in the mountains*. New York: Dutton Children's Books/Penguin.

Rylant, C. (1993). *But I'll be back again*. New York: HarperTrophy/HarperCollins.

Sanders, S. R. (2002). *Crawdad creek*. Washington, DC: National Geographic Society.

Schotter, R. (1997). *Nothing ever happens on 90th Street*. New York: Grolier/Scholastic.

Simon, S. (2000). *From paper airplanes to outer space*. Katonah, NY: Owen.

Taylor, E. (2002). *Nibbles and me*. New York: Simon & Schuster.

Turner, A. (1994). *The Christmas house*. New York: HarperCollins.

Viorst, J. (1987). *The tenth good thing about Barney*. New York: Aladdin/Simon & Schuster.

Viorst, J. (1998). *Rosie and Michael*. New York: Aladdin/Simon & Schuster.

Waber. B. (2002). *Courage*. Boston: Lorraine Books/Houghton Mifflin.

Wiles, D. (2001). *Freedom summer*. New York: Atheneum/Simon & Schuster.

Wollard, K. (1993). *How come? Every kid's science questions explained*. New York: Workman.

Wong, J. S. (2002). *You have to write*. New York: McElderry Books/Simon & Schuster.

Wood, D. (2002). *A quiet place*. New York: Simon & Schuster.

Worth, V. (1994). *All the small poems and fourteen more*. New York: Farrar, Straus and Giroux.

Author

Janet L. Elliott is a literacy trainer for the Center for Literacy Education and Research at Purdue University. In her eighteen years in education, she has taught a variety of grade levels and has worked with teachers and students in grades K–8. She has been a Reading Recovery teacher, a primary literacy trainer and coach, and an intermediate literacy trainer and coach. Elliott has presented on a variety of topics at state and national conferences. She lives with her husband, John, in Indiana, has two grown sons, and loves to spend time with her three young grandsons.

This book was typeset in Palatino and Helvetica by Electronic Imaging.
The typeface used on the cover was Plantagenet Cherokee.
The book was printed on 50-lb. Williamsburg Offset paper
by Midland Information Resources.